METROPOLITAN DECISION PROCESSES

AMERICAN POLITICS RESEARCH SERIES 

METROPOLITAN DECISION PROCESSES

An Analysis of Case Studies

MORRIS DAVIS

MARVIN G. WEINBAUM

UNIVERSITY OF ILLINOIS

RAND McNALLY & COMPANY · Chicago

AMERICAN POLITICS RESEARCH SERIES
Aaron Wildavsky, Series Editor

ALFORD, *Bureaucracy and Participation: Political Cultures in Four Wisconsin Cities*
BARBER, *Power in Committees: An Experiment in the Governmental Process*
CRECINE, *Governmental Problem-Solving: A Computer Simulation of Municipal Budgeting*
DAVIS AND WEINBAUM, *Metropolitan Decision Processes: An Analysis of Case Studies*
DYE, *Politics, Economics, and the Public: Policy Outcomes in the American States*
FRANCIS, *Legislative Issues in the Fifty States: A Comparative Analysis*
KEECH, *The Impact of Negro Voting: The Role of the Vote in the Quest for Equality*
SCHLESINGER, *Ambition and Politics: Political Careers in the United States*
SHARKANSKY, *Spending in the American States*
STEINER, *Social Insecurity: The Politics of Welfare*

Printed in U.S.A. by Rand McNally & Company
Library of Congress Catalog Card Number 69:13291

To

Jonathan and Peter

ACKNOWLEDGMENTS

The first author deeply appreciates the support he received during 1964–65 under Public Health Service Research Grant CH-00098 and during 1965–67 under Grant CH-00201, both from the Division of Community Health Services. One chief benefit of the grants was that they permitted the hiring of two extremely able graduate research assistants, Robert Henry Glick, at Tulane University in 1964–65, and Dennis R. Judd, at the University of Illinois in 1965–67. Mr. Judd, in particular, was a close intellectual companion throughout the development, application, and assessment of our investigative procedures. He combines a clear eye for detail with an ability to see the larger shape of things. A grant from the Bureau of Community Planning at the University of Illinois permitted our keeping Mr. Judd with us for several additional months in 1967. Miss Cheryl L. Mueller was our secretary on this project for more than two years. Besides typing countless drafts of memoranda and chapters, she also helped with many of the tabular compilations. In the closing weeks Miss Linda S. Church came to our assistance and typed most of the final copy. Our wives, Ruth and Francine, have been constant participants in this research project from its original formulation to its final editorial touches. By way of thanks, and as dutiful husbands, we absolve them from all responsibilities for the book they would otherwise rightfully share.

CONTENTS

LIST OF TABLES

INTRODUCTION

THE FULL SCOPE of metropolitan decision-making is obviously too vast for a small book. As a result, we have deliberately posed only a limited array of questions about the subject. For example, do decision activities follow any patterned tempos? Who generally participates in them? How visible are these processes? What is their affective tone? Through what modes do communications predominantly occur, and with what degree of regularity? The descriptions of manifest behavior arising from these sometimes unorthodox inquiries are intended to improve our understanding of the peculiarly process aspects of metropolitan decisions.

Most other approaches to issue conflicts in communities proceed, by contrast, at a molar level. Interest typically rests on such themes as prevailing influence patterns, policy-makers' goals and strategies, and the political structures and rules that channel decision activity. While these concerns do not always slight the kinds of process questions mentioned above, a molecular examination, focusing on discrete units of interaction, holds greater promise of yielding those comparative and quantitative data essential for general theories.

An explicit description and analysis of decision-related activities requires a number of research departures. The change in perspective demands additional interpretive categories, while a meaningful dialogue between researcher and readers necessitates their clear specification. Furthermore, there is the major challenge of revised information needs. Our choice of political case studies as the exclusive source of interaction data is, of course, less innovative than conservative. Case narratives have long supplied vivid and detailed illustrations of men and institutions engaged in shaping public policies. Yet cases have seldom been employed to develop incisive analysis of the very process elements they encompass.

Any effort like ours, which uses case studies comparatively and aggregatively, might appear a direct challenge to current assumptions about the merits of the case method. Indeed, popular opinion holds that while cases are suggestive and educational they are not at present suited to the systematic generation of propositions. The relevance of these judgments to our treatment of case materials, however, is limited. The customary way of reading cases accepts them merely as narratives. From our vantage, though, they provide elemental and numerous interaction units; and it is the statistical applicability of these data that permits us to undertake examinations previously deemed incompatible with the case study genre.

Our premise is that cases furnish a largely untapped store of political behavior, one especially amenable to close interactional analysis. Accordingly, we present findings derived from about 2,800 manifest interactions in some 32 case studies. (In Chapter V, where we group cases by locale and by issue, the figures are somewhat smaller.) None of the narratives is our own composition. Instead, we have selectively drawn studies, most of them familiar and highly regarded, from the standard case literature on community decisions.

The probable adequacy of case materials for an interactional study is, of course, no proof in itself that this way of probing community decisions holds much value. An adequate assessment of the point cannot, in fact, precede the detailed substantive findings of later chapters. All the same, a brief introduction to the several kinds of concerns that preoccupy our analysis should furnish a useful indication of the manner in which we hope to broaden the usual conceptions of metropolitan decision-making.

One important, almost novel, emphasis in our study concerns the pace of issue controversies. Intuitively, it might be imagined that most processes begin rather slowly, gradually gain momentum, and exhibit toward their end a great flurry of interaction. Yet it would be no less reasonable to believe that processes characteristically start with noise and activity, and that the communications rate thereafter decreases as time passes and passions cool. Nor would it be merely fanciful to imagine a U-shaped curve of decision-related interactions, with events clustering thickly at the initiation and conclusion, while the intervening period is far more dormant. More skeptical and perhaps more realistic observers might well consider all these beliefs erroneous. Instead of a single dominant temporal pattern, they might insist that different issue categories and different settings would exhibit distinctive configurations, or even that every decision process is idiosyncratic in its timing.

Whatever the objective truth, three assertions about time as an attribute of metropolitan decisions seem defensible. First, the temporal relationship among events is seldom inconsequential. Indeed, the resources and strategies of actors may be reflected in the timing of their participation. Second, expectations about tempo cannot be confidently deduced from the general maxims of political and social theory. As our discussion has indicated, at least a half dozen inferable patterns possess some logical plausibility. Third, resolution of the problem is unlikely to derive from further speculative rumination. Instead, only a systematically factual examination, or re-examination, of many issue processes can produce credible information about the usual temporal quality of present-day American metropolitan decisions.

In addition to time, our study of interactions looks at the communication modes through which decisions are transacted, the participants in these events, the locales at which they take place, the extent to which they are open to outside scrutiny, their formality or informality of tone, and the degree of their adherence to stable communications networks. Like temporal position, each of these attributes is considered a major aspect of decision processes and an important component of their description.

The modes of communication associated with issue controversies suggest certain crucial relations among decision-makers. The mix of indirect messages and face-to-face meetings often provides considerable evidence about how outcomes are determined and polities are shaped. Many elite power models, for example, assume the prevalence of highly personalized and direct means of interaction. On the contrary, if decision-related communications are customarily transmitted through the press, the range of knowledgeable persons widens, openness pervades the community, and maneuvering that is completely behind-the-scenes and off-the-record likely becomes more difficult and less potent.

Although the question "Who Participates?" may seem less crucial than "Who Governs?," it still occupies a prominent place in decisional analysis. The well-worn concepts of access and initiation testify to its centrality. Nor are the two questions completely separate, since participation of certain kinds, for example, participation that is meaningful, early, on the winning side, or listened to, is often deemed an important indicator of political influence in a community.

To be sure, the aggregation and comparison of participation rates over many decision processes requires our employing rather general classifications of actors. Thus, in this book we speak of elected city officials and not of specific mayors and councilmen, of business and not of particular entrepreneurs and managers. Even broad headings, though, can facilitate useful contrasts among tiers of government or among the business, labor, religious, civil rights, and professional sectors of the polity.

In an analogous manner, attention to the spatial aspect of interactions permits the cataloguing of activities by their occurrence either in, close to, or at a distance from the metropolitan area. Data of this sort are relevant to assessments of both the insularity of local decision processes and their special reliance upon the resources of such external actors as state governments, federal agencies, and large-scale corporations.

The degree of visibility in interactions, e.g., the openness of a public hearing, the partial closure of a council session, the impermeability of a private caucus, is clearly a crucial attribute of issue controversies. The capacity of publics to monitor and to intervene in decisional activities is often a useful index of influence diffusion within the political system. So, too, data indicating the frequency of informal communications like chats and telephone calls, as opposed to more formal communications like petitions and directives, may reveal the ease of access among local interests and also highlight secretive and oligarchical political tendencies in a community.

A comparison of interaction configurations illustrative of preexisting and newly emergent networks with those linking individuals in an idiosyncratic or unprecedented way helps show how far actors who are not ordinarily prominent in decision processes do participate on particular issues. In a like fashion, the distribution of interactions between old and new networks may signify the extent to which decisions are managed by highly exclusive and well-structured groupings rather than by more inclusive arrangements that encompass additional interests.

Our concern with the presence or absence of interaction attributes also extends to their interrelationships. We are particularly interested in those combinations of characteristics that seem on an impressionistic basis most relevant to community decision processes. For example, can we anticipate that the incidence of ephemeral interactions will change as issue controversies mature? Do closed meetings tend to contain stable participant networks, or are they more frequently negotiating sessions among actors not habitually in communication? Are certain non-government interests customarily excluded from informal meetings with government officials? And is this exclusion particularly noticeable in the early or late stages of issue controversies?

A related use of interaction data involves placing the access-related activities of non-government interests on a scale ranging from weak (demonstrations, public statements) through moderate (messages to and from government) to strong (meetings that are simultaneously closed, informal, and regular). This procedure permits various interests to be classified according to their most distinctive forms of political participation. As a result, the relative contributions of business, professional, and labor representatives to the more determinative communications with government can be assessed. One can even compare activity profiles within different temporal stages and thus ascertain not only if business has the closest contacts with government but also if it participates in these intimate sessions earlier on average than other groups.

A further important and obvious application of interaction data is in comparing decision processes among locales and among issues. One is prompted to ask, for example, if various cities employ contrasting means in handling issue controversies. Do they show divergent rates of meetings, messages, and public statements? Do they utilize closed meetings to different degrees or at different stages of decision-making? And do they contrast in their reliance on newly emergent communications networks?

A companion set of questions can be posed about issues. The cases included in our study allow direct examination of decision processes in the fields of housing, urban development, school desegregation, airport location, and water-sanitation facilities. Interactions for these topics, too, may diverge in the dominance of given participants, the devising of policy in formal settings, the impact of ephemeral communications, and so on.

The seven interaction characteristics upon which we focus do not, of course, exhaust the descriptive content of community decision processes. Many other foci are conceivable; indeed, our final chapter specifies several. Taken together, however, the aspects we have emphasized—mode, participants, locale, permeability, formality, continuity, and temporal position—seem pivotal to any thorough understanding of the linkages joining men engaged in decision activities. These characteristics also possess a further advantage in being amenable to systematic coding.

To be sure, substantive relevance is no guarantee of methodological facility, and in operationalizing many of the concepts, we certainly encountered formidable obstacles. The procedural difficulties are well exemplified in the temporal attribute. Throughout this introduction we have used the terms "earlier," "begin," and "the intervening period" as if they have some unimpeachable referents. Clearly, they do not. For all their drama, issue controversies do not come with pre-cut beginnings, middles, and ends, or with numbered acts and scenes. Rules must therefore be devised about when (for our purposes) an issue has proceeded far enough so that we may state that it has begun and, similarly, that it has reached an end point. Techniques must also be stipulated for dividing the resulting time span into several intervals.

Even though all operational translations must to some extent be arbitrary, their utility may seem more salient than their grounding in fiat if they are stated in precise detail, are systematically applied to a diverse selection of materials, and are economical in their retention of available data. We have tried to construct a code of this sort for the seven interaction aspects, one that employs the largest number of classifications compatible with clarity, consistency, and wide application. Only for the tonal attribute of formality were we required to fall back upon a simple dichotomy. For mode, permeability, continuity, and (in practice) locality, tripartite codes are designated. Temporal position involves a six-fold division, while the list of participants we adopted contains more than two dozen headings.

Since our general lines of inquiry and our specific categories both often mark fairly new ways of treating case studies, a considerable portion of this book must be given over to an explanation, and perhaps even a justification, of our approach. For this reason, Chapter I discusses the strengths and weaknesses of the case method and especially its ability to furnish interaction data appropriate for comparative analysis. Chapter II then describes the research procedures used throughout the remainder of our study, setting forth in some detail the various categories and classifications applied to each interaction unit.

The next three chapters contain our specific findings, together with propositional summaries. Chapter III provides a serial overview of the seven attributes within the entire case sample, Chapter IV considers some of the relationships that obtain among these aspects, and Chapter V examines individual cities and issues in order to isolate their more particular decisional components.

In Chapter VI we look first at ways process analysis might be readily improved and then at the compatibility of an interaction emphasis with other theoretical concerns among students of community politics. In addition, we investigate the relevance of our findings to approaches already familiar in urban political research. As already noted, our emphasis is not upon institutions, norms, or power. Yet, we believe each of these alternative themes could profit from the introduction of process descriptions. To make this assertion more plausible, we consider in turn the kinds of interaction aspects that are likely to be associated with municipal reform institutions, with various dominant community norms, and with pyramidal or polyarchic distributions of power.

One last point that relates to our use of the term metropolitan decisions ought perhaps to be made explicit before we turn to our data base, methods, and findings. We consider the term to include all decisions that occur anywhere in the metropolitan area, provided the government of the central city has a major stake in the outcome and the substance of the issue controversy is salient to a considerable fraction of the area's population. Often, of course, these issues involve not only the central city but also the county, the suburbs, or the state, so that they are metropolitan in an interjurisdictional sense as well. But we do not exclude narratives that take place completely within the central city. Hopefully, our choice of the phrase metropolitan decisions will not disturb most readers. If anyone does deem it peculiar, though, he should merely consider it a shorthand label for "important political decisions for major American cities."

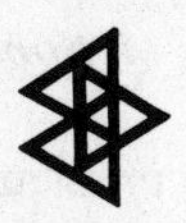

CHAPTER I

Infirmity and Efficacy in the Case Method

ANY REFERENCE TO *the* case method, as in the title of this chapter, is likely to be misleading. Cases are not exclusively the tool of any single discipline. Indeed, some of the larger format differences among cases can be explained by their service in such disparate fields as medicine, law, and business administration. Even within political science the case approach eludes easy definition, because it serves a variety of ends, four of which will shortly be specified in some detail.

VARIETY IN CASE USES

Generally, cases in medicine are working tools; those in law, authoritative guides; and those in business administration, pedagogic instruments. In medicine, and analogously in social work, case histories and case reports contain details about a patient's past condition and current progress. The information is practical, with the case writer ordinarily a participant in the process he observes and records. At the same time, an assemblage of similar cases, under accepted medical procedures, can further the profession's understanding of disease and infection.

Law cases are typically less descriptive than medical reports. Almost invariably, the judicial decisions they contain adhere to logical or rhetorical styles of expression. As in medicine, though, a practical application is readily apparent. Indeed, law cases contain critical guides to statutory interpretation, legal precepts, and predilections of courts and judges.

Business cases are more exclusively pedagogic. In simulating crucial problem-solving situations, students are obliged to ponder sets of alternatives and to recognize and evaluate thereby the adequacy of their information, the nature of their goals, and the implications of their actions. Unlike law cases, these narratives are neither purposefully authoritative nor visibly laden with principles. Though they may also implant values, their chief purpose is to propagate skills among students.[1]

It is easy to conclude that case studies in political science resemble each of the foregoing in some ways and not in others, but it is difficult to find precisely wherein the similarities and differences reside. A chief reason for tentativeness is that the forms and purposes of political cases are still rather hazily conceived. To some, in fact, they can include any focused presentations that deal mainly in particulars.[2] In these pages we follow more customary practice and limit the term to that portion of literature in which political events and issue controversies are re-created in a reasonably narrative manner. Even here a rapid overview reveals at least four aims that case materials support. These objectives are not mutually exclusive, and most cases contribute to more than one, but they are sufficiently distinct to warrant separate discussion.

Political cases are often used to reconstruct "the whole story." Topics are chosen, in part, because of their intrinsic interest to the discipline or because of their notoriety.[3] By amassing a great body of information and identifying to some extent the complex of connective forces, the case authors attempt to bring order to chaos. Their major emphasis, though, is on producing coherent narratives and not on exploring themes and eliciting principles. The most proficient authors in the genre strive to go beyond formalistic data, but in so doing they frequently are obliged to utilize impressionistic materials or interpret motives and perceptions. Often the result is a story with both strong verisimilitude and uncertain historical authenticity.

[1] On the case method in these three disciplines see Harold Stein, ed., *Public Administration and Policy Development* (New York: Harcourt, Brace, 1952), pp. xx–xxi.

[2] Lane *et al.* state that political science cases "represent the juxtaposition of a statement of a theory or problem and a description of a situation." Robert E. Lane, James D. Barber, and Fred I. Greenstein, *An Introduction to Political Analysis,* 4th ed. (Englewood Cliffs, N.J.: Prentice-Hall, 1967), p. iv. Sociologists, too, employ "case" in a highly inclusive manner. See, for example, Terry N. Clark, "Comparability in Community Research," a paper presented at the Sixth World Congress of Sociology, International Sociological Association, Evian, France, September 1966.

[3] Political case literature contains many accounts that carefully document landmark events. One outstanding example is Corinne Silverman's "The Little Rock Story," in Edwin A. Bock and Alan K. Campbell, eds., *Case Studies in American Government* (Englewood Cliffs, N.J.: Prentice-Hall, 1962), pp. 1–46. Steven K. Bailey's classic case about the Employment Act of 1946, *Congress Makes a Law* (New York: Columbia University Press, 1950), also captures an important moment in political history even as it illustrates significant phases of the legislative process.

The design of many political cases best serves instructional ends. Though in a loose sense this may be true of them all, some are especially useful as teaching aids. By introducing a student to the web of events and the intricacies of political choice, case studies hopefully increase his understanding, spur his interest, and enable him to avoid simplistic conceptions.[4] Particular emphasis is given in some classes to the students' vicariously playing central roles in the decision process. In this way cases may furnish practical prescriptions by example as well as incisive tools for probing political institutions and forces.[5]

Cases may provide concrete illustrations of major themes in political science. Indeed, most case studies concerned with legislative processes, interest group activity, and judicial decision-making are explicitly fashioned for this purpose. Through them concepts like committee autonomy, differential access, and the use of precedent become more vivid. Too often, perhaps, themes are treated unsystematically, and analyses are just appended to narratives rather than integrated with them. Still, very frequently cases best permit insight into the operations and functional interrelationships of key political institutions.[6]

Finally, there is a small number of case studies, usually in collections, specifically intended to generate and refine propositions. Banfield's series of issue-centered cases in Chicago furnishes an empirical basis for his perceptive observations about policy-making in that city. Altshuler's examination of planning decisions in the Minneapolis-St. Paul area integrates case data and theoretical constructs even more closely. Perhaps the most rigorous instance of narrative and proposition intertwined in a case study is the account by Snyder and Paige of the U.S. decision to intervene

[4] Tillett's enthusiasm for this application is noteworthy. "Considered as teaching materials, case studies offer many advantages to the student. They take him where they find him, at the level of common sense, and build upon his ordinary understanding of the actions of human beings, involve him in a story of considerable human interest, and present political problems as they are perceived by political actors and ordinary spectators. It is hoped the approach will do more than merely interest the student, though in practice it seems cases perform this function well." Paul Tillett, "Case Studies in Practical Politics: Their Use and Abuse," a paper presented at the Annual Meeting of the American Political Science Association, Washington, D.C., 1959.

[5] Several of the cases in the Stein collection comfortably fall into this category. "The Sale of the Tankers" and "The Kings River Project" both illustrate well how such accounts can re-create the steps leading to public policy decisions.

[6] Probably the most common aim of political case studies is just this sort of subject-area elucidation. Marvin A. Harder, *Nonpartisan Election: A Political Illusion?* (New York: Holt, 1958) and many other publications in the Eagleton Institute Series clearly serve that function; so also do the seven cases in Alan F. Westin, ed., *The Uses of Power* (New York: Harcourt, Brace and World, 1962). See also Richard T. Frost, ed., *Cases in State and Local Government* (Englewood Cliffs, N.J.: Prentice-Hall, 1961), though some of its rather short accounts are at most semi-narrative.

in Korea. In all three works the flow of events does not merely exemplify theories: it aids in their construction.[7]

Despite this multiplicity of purposes, or perhaps because of it, the political case has failed thus far to win full acceptance as an analytic device. Criticisms lodged against it are frequently well founded, even if some of the deficiencies are not its problem exclusively. Probably the most serious indictment charges that the case technique typically fails to furnish systematically comparable materials. What is obviously lacking is a set of practicable and rigorous analytic units in terms of which case materials can be consistently manipulated. To this end, a scheme of analysis that rests upon observable interaction behavior in cases is described in our first two chapters and employed in the following three.

CRITICISM AND DEFENSE OF CASES

Our first task is to examine briefly reservations that have been expressed about the potential contribution of case studies to political analysis. Most of these criticisms fasten upon either dramatic tone, research procedures, or social-scientific relevance.

Objections to the exciting style and content of many cases can be easily countered. That cases may make vivid reading is not in itself a demonstration of their unreliability. Nor is the usual reliance of case writers on highly visible and memorable events a unique failing in political research. Those who analyze roll calls in the House of Representatives or who scale decisions of the Supreme Court similarly focus upon readily ascertainable and ceremonial data. Furthermore, throughout political life behavior is not necessarily less crucial for being more manifest.

Criticisms aimed at the research methods of case writers are frequently more serious. Many of their data resources, especially from official documents and newspaper accounts, are superficial or misleading. Other information is often haphazardly selected and laced with imaginative reconstructions. Impressionistic and "inside dopester" evidence, too, may be employed quite freely. Political case writers, indeed, seem to possess no clear standards for including or excluding materials or assign-

[7] Edward C. Banfield, *Political Influence* (New York: Free Press, 1961), Alan A. Altshuler, *The City Planning Process* (Ithaca: Cornell University Press, 1965), and Richard C. Snyder and Glenn D. Paige, "The United States Decision to Resist Aggression in Korea," *Administrative Science Quarterly,* 3 (1958), 341–78. Other recent and ambitious attempts to construct systematic categories from case materials include Frederick C. Mosher, ed., *Governmental Reorganizations* (Indianapolis: Bobbs-Merrill, 1967), Aaron Wildavsky, *Leadership in a Small Town* (Totawa, N.J.: Bedminster Press, 1964), and Robert L. Crain, *The Politics of School Desegregation* (Chicago: Aldine, 1968).

ing them relative weights. This is a serious failing and one to which we devote some attention in our concluding chapter. Problems of selectivity, though, are scarcely confined to case writing. No descriptive approach, however tight its conceptual scheme, is invulnerable to that sort of criticism.

Finally, political science cases are often indicted for their meager contribution to the theoretical side of the discipline. Their rich contextual data are usually believed to contribute little to generalizations about political phenomena. Though cases often describe important and interesting events—for example, a decision to build American military bases in Spain or a dispute between a central city and its adjacent suburbs over water resources—they typically furnish no satisfying means for extending findings beyond particular circumstance. Narratives thus appear hemmed in by their peculiar facts and, except for intuitive extrapolations, unique.[8]

Despite their apparent severity, these three charges are neither unprecedented in magnitude nor sufficient to show that reliable and systematically examined case materials are impossible. Objections on the grounds of representativeness—asking about the relationship between a recorded story and events in the real world—raise no problems not encountered to some extent in any selective portrait of empirical activity. While the criticism of theoretical incapacity is understandable, given the predominant uses to which political cases have hitherto been put, we are not without practicable means to overcome much of this deficiency. In fact, the apparently unsystematic character of political cases can be transmuted into an important theoretical strength.

Almost invariably, human interaction is the cohesive substance of case narratives. Different studies may stress different considerations, for example, the strategic concerns of actors, the impact of surrounding political and social forces, and the relevance of institutionalized behavior patterns. Whatever the emphasis, however, underneath are the interactions of men, usually organized in the process of making decisions and resolving conflicts. Obviously, case studies are not complete and precise

[8] Since political scientists who find little or no value in the case method have usually refrained from criticizing it in detail, the limitations of the approach have been enunciated principally by its occasional practitioners and not by its most severe detractors. Among the most cogent assessments are Dwight Waldo, "Five Perspectives in the Cases of the Inter-University Case Program" and James W. Fesler, "The Case Method in Political Science," both in Edwin A. Bock, ed., *Essays on the Case Method in Public Administration* (Brussels: International Institute of Administrative Sciences, 1962), Tillet, "Case Studies in Practical Politics," Roscoe C. Martin, Frank J. Munger, *et al., Decisions in Syracuse* (Bloomington: Indiana University Press, 1961), ch. 1, and Herbert Kaufman, "The Next Step in Case Studies," *Public Administration Review,* 18 (1958), 52–59.

inventories of interpersonal activity. Furthermore, they typically avoid such sophisticated tools for studying social dynamics as attitudinal scales, ecological mapping, and depth interviews. They compensate for these probable deficiencies, though, by being eclectically inclusive. In fact, their most telling characteristic is "rawness." Except for being ordered more or less chronologically, events are usually not severely rearranged by case authors. It is this availability of plentiful and relatively untreated interaction data that makes political cases especially well suited to secondary analyses.[9]

Uncovering these data and discerning their patterns should yield important insights into decision processes. After all, as Jennings remarks, "Interaction is the common medium for exerting interpersonal influence."[10] Analyses of metropolitan cases thus can facilitate an understanding of the way large and complex communities fashion policies and resolve conflicts. Systematic use of interaction data should also increase the probability of successfully aggregating and comparing decisions across locales and among issues.

Admittedly, our examination of case study content detects only quite gross relationships. A focus upon observable communications[11] also provides few clues about the motives, values, and base resources of actors. What a careful study of interactions can do is facilitate the identification of groups and individuals that come into the decisional arena, make demands, and reach accommodations. As such, it should help us comprehend the forms and contexts of participation by providing a rough but serviceable sketch of the concrete behavioral structures manifested in community decision-making.

[9] Stein recognizes this advantage when he writes that "the more neatly the materials of history are cut to a particular pre-determined pattern, the more sharply defined and therefore limited the uses that can be made of the account. For it is a significant phenomenon of the social sciences generally that an account based on careful observation unconfined by the limitations of a rigorously defined thesis can be fruitfully re-examined by successive readers using different methods of analysis and coming to different kinds of conclusions." *Op. cit.*, p. xxvi.

[10] M. Kent Jennings, *Community Influentials* (New York: Free Press, 1964), p. 72.

[11] Throughout this study the terms "interaction" and "communication" are employed interchangeably. For other theoretical purposes, of course, it may be useful to distinguish them. Thus, according to Blau and Scott, "The concept of social interaction focuses principally upon the formal characteristics of social relation: such terms as frequency, initiative, superordination, and reciprocity indicate its dimensions. The concept of communication, on the other hand, directs attention to the meaningful context conveyed in the encounter, and its characteristics are described by such terms as flow of messages, obstacles, positive and negative reactions, and exchange." (Peter M. Blau and W. Richard Scott, *Formal Organizations* [San Francisco: Chandler, 1962], p. 116). Since, as the next chapter makes clear, our coding procedure lights upon both types of phenomena, there is no need to adopt one or the other term exclusively.

THE UNIT EMPLOYED

As it will soon become apparent, to isolate and identify interaction units in political case studies is no simple task. Frequently, information must be teased from the narratives. In addition, the analyst may at times feel that his interaction data are largely a function of the case writers' literary styles, dominant interests, and available funds of knowledge. Moreover, the manifest content of a case imposes limitations, since going very far behind the printed word, inferring ignored materials, or supplementing accounts from outside sources can result only in a fictionalized quasi-case. Even so, the analyst is not totally a captive of his materials. He is not at all precluded from selectively reexamining case content in order to extract meaningful units of information.

Two examples will illustrate not only the kinds of interactions that have been identified and analyzed but also those that lie too far below the surface to be uncovered.[12] The first quotation is from the classic case study "Moses on the Green."

> The next day a delegation from the neighborhood went to see Deputy
> 1 Mayor John J. Theobald with the request that work on the project be held up pending further study. Theobald promised to see what could be done, but the delegates left with a sense of frustration. . . .
>
> While the group was meeting with Theobald, Moses announced to the
> 2 newspapers that work on the project would recommence the following day, April 19. But no equipment appeared on the 19th, and instead
> 3 Moses stated that he would wait out the opposition. The neighborhood
> 4 was elated at this apparent victory. Newman announced: "It appears we have Moses stopped cold." But on Friday, April 20, a small piece of construction equipment appeared on the scene. Mrs. Newman, however, had organized a watch system in the Park during the daylight hours, and
> 5 the equipment was blocked by two women and a child.[13]

Each interaction, identified by a number in the margin, is readily detected. The first comprises a meeting between the neighborhood residents and Deputy Mayor John Theobald. The second is a public announcement by Robert Moses. A subsequent announcement by Moses constitutes the third interaction. The fourth is a public statement by spokesmen for the neighborhood group, while the fifth involves joint action by two unnamed women and a child.

[12] Other aspects of the code procedure are described in Chapter II and in the Appendix of this volume.

[13] John B. Keeley, "Moses on the Green," in Edwin A. Bock, ed., *State and Local Government: A Case Book* (University, Ala.: University of Alabama Press, 1963), pp. 29–30.

A gimlet eye might discern two other latent references to interactions in the citation, but neither of them, we believe, can be coded. One reads that "the neighborhood was elated" after Moses' second announcement. Perhaps that state of mind arose only after many communications. Individuals may have attended meetings and statements may have been issued, the result being the summary designation "elated" by the author. But surely, without more detailed information than we possess, it would be unwise to reach such conclusions.

Would we be on safer ground in counting as an interaction Mrs. Newman's organization of the watch system? In all probability many events preceded the picketing that we record. There may have been telephone calls and even preparatory meetings. Again, though, we have no concrete information about this probable set of events. Since our substantive analyses seek to describe actual structures of communication, we find ourselves obliged to ignore those that are merely possible. Any other tactic would surely result in vast numbers of pseudo-facts being read into narratives.

A quotation from Mowitz and Wright's *Profile of a Metropolis* indicates some further problems of identification.

> A handful of Sterling Township residents were on hand at the Michigan
> 1 Aeronautics Commission meeting on September 13. The commission politely heard their brief and unorganized protests and then proceeded to approve unanimously Detroit's request for a northeast airport. The
> 2 Macomb County Board of Supervisors and the school board of the city
> 3 of Utica, on the northern border of Sterling Township, voted approval of the proposed airport. Packer, recalling these local endorsements, gave much of the credit to McElroy who "helped us tremendously on the Sterling
> 4 Township site." Favorable responses were also forthcoming from the
> 5 CAA officials who were consulted informally.[14]

Once again, some of the interactions—those indicated by numbers in the margin—are easily coded. The first three involve meetings of public bodies, in one instance with area residents explicitly in attendance. The last two interactions, an official message from CAA officials and an earlier informal communique between the Detroit Aviation Commission[15] and the CAA, are also fairly evident. But, as in the first quotation, there is also more difficult language.

For example, how should Packer's statement be treated? Conceivably, it may be a remark quoted in the press and conveyed to the public. The tone of its recounting, however, suggests that it is a recollec-

[14] Robert J. Mowitz and Deil S. Wright, *Profile of a Metropolis* (Detroit: Wayne State University Press, 1962), p. 395.

[15] Earlier paragraphs make it clear that the Detroit Aviation Commission was a party to those prior communiques.

tion, probably told to the researcher long after the event. If so, it does not constitute an interaction within the ambit of the case described. As for the favorable responses by the CAA, they were probably issued only after considerable discussions within the agency and perhaps even between it and various organs of state and local government. For all one's suspicion, though, there is no convincing way to infer anything sure beyond the manifest communication from the CAA that we do record.

JUSTIFYING THE APPROACH

Imposing a consistent analytic scheme on materials not designed for comparison obviously poses difficulties. Particularly toward the day's end, the coder is likely to feel that the narratives are hopelessly incomplete, purposefully vague, and larded with irrelevant asides. Yet their use still offers many advantages. Written, as they usually are, by individuals closely familar with local practices and privy to information that might either have been denied to us originally or that has since become unavailable, cases provide a wealth of decision data otherwise beyond our reach. Full accounts of communications networks, of course, are neither theoretically possible nor empirically parsimonious. But so long as the samples of interaction in these narratives are not grossly and systematically biased, they constitute valuable documentation for generalizing about political behavior, and far better documentation than in most other sources.[16]

Certain kinds of political cases, of course, lend themselves more easily to interaction analysis than others. Narratives that sketch processes broadly are less useful than those that carefully depict the modes, participants, and contexts of interpersonal communication. Case studies that fictionalize, collapse, or grossly reorganize interaction data—tactics that may accord well with various pedagogic goals—usually are not compatible with our approach either. So long as interactions are closely described, however, it matters little whether the narrations are intended to tell stories, illustrate themes, or furnish the bases for subsequent theories. Given our scheme of analysis, it is the codability of cases, rather than the purposes intended by the authors, that is relevant.

These caveats and limitations should not obscure the fact that our method permits generalizations to be formed on the basis of a sizable

[16] Collections of studies about decision-making in a single community have recently become an important part of the case literature. Five of the most successful series are Mowitz and Wright, *Profile of a Metropolis,* Martin, Munger, *et al., Decisions in Syracuse,* Banfield, *Political Influence,* Wildavsky, *Leadership in a Small Town,* and Mills and Davis, *Small City Government* (New York: Random House, 1962). In each book the narratives that describe various community issues "hold constant" many crucial institutional factors and many important political participants. Consequently, a focus on even one political setting allows some limited generalizations about decision processes within that locality. See also Chapter V of this volume.

number of cases. It also allows us to go somewhat further than those few authors who have previously striven to make metropolitan case studies the foundation for their concept building. For despite their sophistication in data handling, writers like Banfield and Altshuler have sought mainly to elicit propositions *from* case materials. Their narratives suggest to them insights and hypotheses, but the critical tests are presumably left to other procedures. In contrast, the approach employed here fixes upon relationships generated by the narratives themselves. While further testing in order to establish their external validity remains valuable,[17] all the propositions advanced are imminent *within* the case data examined.

Once mined and processed, the plentitude of interactions in cases permits the avoidance of a particularly vexing problem in political science, namely, the infrequency and incomparability of phenomena most germane to the discipline. This difficulty has led to the bifurcation of political science into primarily "micro" and "macro" subfields, the former applying sophisticated methods to data that are often only marginally political, the latter employing discursive means to interpret momentous political events. An escape from the dilemma lies in retaining the large units but analyzing them into components. Such a strategy has recently been used in cross-national political studies.[18] Isolating the behavioral units within metropolitan case studies and identifying various of their aspects should similarly facilitate comparison and understanding, despite a restricted complement of political case studies. Indeed, it may furnish the only means for coherently comprehending decision processes in a multitude of urban settings.

Hopefully, our aims and procedures in the following chapters will seem reasonable. But if they do, the reader may think it odd that so little effort has previously been expended on treating metropolitan case materials comparatively, especially given the continual interest of political scientists in the processes of decision-making. Much of this inactivity, we believe, can be traced to an uncritical acceptance of assumptions about case study limitations. Even more crucially, identification and analysis of behavioral regularities across cases has had to await a feasible analytic framework and an objective basis for quantitative assessment.

[17] External validity, "the confidence with which the findings can be generalized to populations and measures beyond those immediately studied," is discussed with much subtlety in Eugene J. Webb, Donald T. Campbell, Richard D. Schwartz, and Lee Sechrest, *Unobtrusive Measures* (Chicago: Rand McNally, 1966), chs. 1 and 7. The quotation is on p. 172.

[18] Banks and Textor, for example, specify almost 200 dichotomized characteristics for up to 115 independent countries. The thousands of two-by-two cross tabulations they then generate is ample evidence that, even though nation-states are severely limited in number, sufficient grist obtains for a genuinely cross-national mill. Arthur S. Banks and Robert B. Textor, *A Cross-Polity Survey* (Cambridge: M.I.T. Press, 1963).

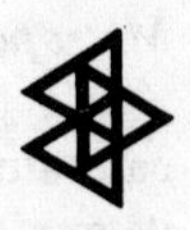

CHAPTER II

A Strategy for Systemization

TO ANALYZE METROPOLITAN decision-making in the manner suggested by the previous chapter requires an investigative method that is both sensitive and rigorous. Only a carefully designed interpretive scheme can hope to extract and order interaction data from individual case narratives and thus provide the basis for comparisons across a variety of decision processes. A suitable approach must accommodate widely different reportorial styles, topical concerns, and conceptual assumptions so that each case will reveal its key actors, the linkages between them, and the contexts of their behavior. In addition, the techniques utilized should produce information copious and consistent enough to warrant quantitative treatment.

These aims are not unrealistic, but they are formidable. Because subjective judgment in identifying and interpreting interactions cannot be wholly exorcised, special efforts must be made to assure systematic and reliable categorization. At the same time, every effort possible must be exerted to retain the substantive richness of case materials. Although comparative analyses may occasion a high level of abstraction and thereby sacrifice much of the glinting color of the original narratives, coded data should not be wholly severed from the cases that give them life. Finally, the approach selected should draw upon and, hopefully, extend current theories about political influence and community decision-making.

AN ANALYTIC SCHEME

In accordance with the preceding requirements, an analytic scheme is presented here that isolates and characterizes the interaction content of case studies. For each interaction identified, an assessment is made of its mode, actors, spatial location, permeability, formality, continuity, and temporal position. Although the complete code employed can be found in the Appendix, it is useful here briefly to set forth the principal categories and the reasoning that underlies their use.

Three *modes* of interaction are distinguished. Meetings are proximate, whereas messages and public statements involve communication at a distance. Clearly, these modes vary in many respects. For example, meetings are often characterized by flexible interplay among participants, while (except perhaps for telephone calls) messages and public statements generally remain fixed during their transmission. Messages, which typically show alternating responses among determinate actors, also differ markedly from public statements, with their one-way disseminations. It is possible to imagine special situations that would partake of all three categories,[1] but these scarcely appear in the case materials.

Because of our comparative aims, there is little point in recording specific individuals or their affiliated institutions. Instead, our concern is with *actor roles.* Role is interpreted according to the office an individual holds or, lacking that, the interest he supposedly represents. Unless a person explicitly plays two roles, neither of which can be assigned primacy, he is coded only once in any single interaction. Thus, a businessman who is elected to a board of supervisors is recorded solely as a county official when he attends meetings of the board or when he speaks as a supervisor.[2] Were he to be simultaneously appointed to a city-county building authority, he would, when acting in that capacity, be coded as a member of a local intergovernmental board and not as a spokesman for business or an elected county official. This convention surely simplifies reality, since a person may at the same time wear many hats, but it has the virtue of not requiring more knowledge about the affiliations of persons than the little supplied by most texts.[3]

[1] For example, a televised discussion among panelists located in Europe and America may simultaneously involve messages by satellite and public statements to audiences at home as well as immediate encounters by some of the participants.

[2] One actor code is used for each kind of role in evidence during an interaction, no matter how many persons are playing it. This convention, necessary because one often has only approximate information about numbers of participants, has the desirable effect of obviating duplicate coding. Note, however, that because of its salience and complexity in most metropolitan case studies, the domain of government has been subdivided rather finely.

[3] Two other advantages of this non-plural coding procedure might also be mentioned in passing. First, it obviates guessing which, among an individual's various allegiances and reference groups, are decisive at a given moment. Second, it alone enables us to record collegial bodies like councils and legislatures, where our ignorance extends additionally to individual members' attendance at given interactions.

Spatial location is classified under four headings. The first includes the central city in each case study and the immediate intrastate environs. The second encompasses locales elsewhere within the state, while the third refers to any interaction site outside it. Last, an indeterminate category is employed, chiefly because for most public statements the locus of receivers cannot be meaningfully specified.[4]

Permeability of interaction boundaries is divided into three classifications. The first applies to interactions that, either in their nature or by deliberate intent, are restricted to small numbers of participants. The second includes encounters and communiques that are neither hidden from larger audiences nor dominated by them. The third embraces interactions that are in fact attended by, or made manifest to, considerable numbers of persons, often heterogeneous or ill defined, most of whom can be characterized as outsiders or at best occasional participants in the core process being described. A caucus by city council members, an ordinary meeting of the council, and a noisy and provocative council hearing illustrate in turn the three levels of permeability delineated here. Further examples would be a memorandum circulated only among the staff of a housing commission, a report to the city council by the commission, and a press statement issued by it.

In regard to *formality*, interactions are dichotomized into those that are highly structured and recorded for the public record and those that are more spontaneous and off-the-record. The former include official decision-making sessions, notifications of authoritative action, and public statements. The latter encompass privileged communications and behind-the-scenes maneuvering, whether within the staff of a single agency or among persons representing various organizations and interests.

Continuity in interaction patterning is differentiated at three levels. Many of the communications specified in a narrative exemplify networks that predate the case and will undoubtedly postdate it. But new relationships, too, may be occasioned by an issue controversy and be repeated with sufficient regularity to constitute a genuine and novel interaction network. Finally, the role configuration of a meeting, message, or public statement may be ephemeral, being both limited to a given decision process and unusual even then. Classifying interactions into those that follow old channels, those that signal new ones, and those that lie apart

[4] Separate encodings are performed for senders and for receivers in classifying both the actor roles and the locations applicable to messages and public statements. (Indeterminate locations appear very infrequently in our analyses, since attention is placed chiefly on the locus of senders rather than receivers.) The remaining aspects of such interactions at a distance, and all components of meetings, require only single code lists.

from well-worn courses helps one capture a crucial aspect of communication processes.

QUARTILE MAPPING

The last aspect of interaction with which we are concerned, its temporal position, is so central to our presentation in Chapters III and IV that it warrants separate treatment here.[5] In addition, the special methods employed in assessing this characteristic probably deserve an extended discussion.

For many reasons we are interested in knowing whether various sorts of interactions occur quite early in an issue controversy, somewhat before or somewhat after its midpoint, or close to its conclusion. To illustrate, do certain categories of actors appear on the scene particularly early or particularly late? Are closed meetings more characteristic of the middle stages of a metropolitan case than of its beginning and ending? Do ephemeral communications occur at noticeably different rates as cases proceed in time? Are encounters that are simultaneously informal and fully permeable (e.g., demonstrations) most likely to occur during a particular phase in decision-making?

In order to answer these and similar questions, we require a scheme that permits us to assign beginning and ending dates to each case and to divide the intervening span of time into stages of similar duration. Because we are comparing data across (as well as within) case studies, relative temporal units are obviously more useful than absolute ones. After all, even a cursory inspection of narratives shows that their decision processes may last anywhere from a few days to many years. Preliminary manipulations of the case data, with considerable trial and error, have led us to conclude that division of time spans into four phases, which we have appropriately labeled quartiles, provides us with the optimum of reliably specified temporal information.

Obviously, more finely cut data would be desirable. One can imagine, for example, an interesting sequential analysis that would relate interactions to those that follow them immediately or by some designated lag. Responses to stimuli and the stimulation of subsequent responses could thus be isolated. Such an approach, however, would require data more precise than even the most careful writers of cases normally provide. Unfortunate though it may be, a rough device like quartiles fits the available

[5] In Chapter V, where our sample sizes are considerably reduced, and where the additional control of city or issue is used, temporal analysis necessarily receives much less attention.

materials better than more elegant schemes, just as in a meat market a cleaver is more appropriate than a scalpel.

The necessity for approximate tools is apparent even in the dating of individual interactions. Narratives may identify their temporal position quite precisely, but often we are told merely that the interactions occurred "during the next month" or "in 1957." Usually inferences by interpolation can be made in ordering communications, but it is far easier to assign them to quartiles than to rank them precisely. Furthermore, if a series of similar interactions is alluded to in such a way that its items cannot be readily separated,[6] in counting the sequence by convention as a single interaction one can assign it only approximate and general time limits.

If we are to cut narratives into four pieces, though, we must first decide where they begin and end. Clusters of events in the real world admittedly do not come with labels like beginning and end attached to them, but writers do enter at some point and leave off at a later one, and it might seem reasonable to adopt their choices as our temporal bounds. In practice, however, this tactic will not do. Because authors frequently present a brief historical sketch as prologue to their main narrative, and because they often append a similarly sketchy epilogue, such a strategy would grossly extend the outer limits of most cases and would result in quartiles of equal time being quite insensitive to the periodicities of interaction. Other pleasant and easy ways of avoiding this problem also seem barred to us: not all authors indicate by subheadings or the like how far their prologues and epilogues extend, nor is it possible to seek from the data obvious take-off points that distinguish the main bulk of the narrative from the preliminaries that precede it or the literary touches that round it out.

Under these circumstances our chosen procedure has been to eliminate consistently given proportions of interactions from both temporal ends of a narrative. We then stipulate that for analytic purposes a case commences only after a requisite percentage of interactions has passed and that it concludes similarly with a certain percentage of interactions yet to come. The technique employed is simply to count the number of interactions, each having an identical unit value in the count, and then to eliminate the first 10 per cent and the last 5 per cent.[7] The time span

[6] One may read, for example, that "committee hearings were held frequently during the spring and summer" or that "letters and telephone calls poured in from residents that week."

[7] The aesthetics of symmetry might seem to argue for an equivalent cut at either end, but observation quickly shows that case studies generally contain leaner epilogues than prologues. Consequently, a second identical cut would be excessive.

encompassed by the remaining 85 per cent of interactions includes all the case materials to be analyzed.

The temporal flow that the latter interactions encompass can then be divided into four periods of equal duration.[8] These quartiles permit us to make comparisons from case to case no matter what their absolute length, just as age-sex pyramids facilitate demographic comparisons among populations of different magnitudes. Indeed, without some temporal frame of this kind, concerns like those with which this section began would defy systematic study.

FEASIBILITY AND THEORETICAL RELEVANCE

The seven aspects of interaction used here and their distinguishing characteristics can be defended on grounds of both feasibility and theoretical significance. The second criterion is more vital and worthy of more detailed discussion, but the first is hardly unimportant in a world whose phenomena are often reported in diverse and uncoordinated ways.

As we have already emphasized, the use of quartile rather than sequential analysis stems from limitations in the case materials. A second, perhaps less obvious, example is the treatment of public statements as interactions. Undoubtedly, such pronouncements—a press release by an airline, a speech by the mayor, a news story quoting a businessman, an open letter by an aroused citizen—do constitute part of the informational ambiance that pervades a community. The frequently evident presence of public statements and the ease with which they may be collected does not, however, lessen their substantive formalism. Coding them and including them in analyses leaves one open to a charge of stressing outer appearances at the expense of more fundamental realities within.[9]

[8] In three case studies more than 90 per cent of the interactions fell within a single time period. That span was itself then treated as the entire narrative to be analyzed and was divided into four new quartiles. The three accounts handled by this alternate method are Gladfelter-Water, Logue-Demotion, and Rossi-Hyde Park. For further information on them see Table III.1.

[9] A previous study (Morris Davis, "Some Aspects of Detroit's Decisional Profile," *Administrative Science Quarterly,* 12 [1967], 209–24) attempted to avoid these objections by coding not public statements but instead earlier meetings that could be imputed from them. A press release by an information officer of a company, for example, implied an earlier gathering of company officials. This procedure, however, was often interpretively awkward. Though by convention each statement was assumed to indicate a single meeting of a relevant organization, one knows that many announcements are preceded by no meetings and that others are formulated only after a long series of them. Furthermore, it often proved difficult to determine that persons with group affiliations were communicating at the request of those groups and not just on their own. For these and similar reasons the analytic scheme resulted in findings several removes from the case data and suspect in both validity and reliability.

The use of broad categories for all interactions aspects, with the possible exception of role, can similarly be justified by the frequently sparse data in case studies. Surely, more precise differentiations in permeability can be imagined than closed, partly open, and fully open. Surely, the scale of communications continuity includes meaningful positions other than the three—regular, case patterned, and ephemeral—we have designated. Even these gross categories, though, permitted some choices to be made only after conferences among the coders. Indeed, we were sorely tempted to provide a "don't know" alternative for each aspect.[10]

Besides considerations of feasibility, our procedures reflect a wish to produce findings of theoretical interest. Three examples will serve to show how our approaches fit within more general concerns of political science and adjacent social sciences. First, and most generally, emphasis is placed upon the structure and process of communications in metropolitan settings. Such a focus appears particularly useful in studying complex associations and decision flows. Indeed, attention to the "nerves" of a system seems now to be taking precedence over older core notions such as power and groups.[11]

Second, our classification of actors is consonant with most role theories. The version adopted here stresses the organizational affiliation of an individual. It fastens upon the position held (or, in lieu of actual position, the interest represented), which accounts for a person's participation in a given interaction. While in office, a mayor is coded as an elected city official. Once his term is over, he reverts to being a businessman, a professional, or whatever best describes his current status.[12] Conversely, interaction between a mayor and a high-level city administrator is always considered part of a regular network. A newly elected mayor

[10] For the usual reasons this escape mechanism was ruled out: the category would probably balloon, and there would still be the difficulty of establishing points at which a characteristic becomes so unclear one cannot tell what code level properly applies.

[11] Among the most immediately political studies built upon a communications basis are Raymond A. Bauer, Ithiel de Sola Pool, and Lewis A. Dexter, *American Business and Public Policy* (New York: Atherton, 1963), Karl W. Deutsch, *The Nerves of Government* (New York: Free Press, 1963), and William J. Gore, *Administrative Decision-Making* (New York: Wiley, 1964). Works of a more speculative nature, e.g., Richard L. Meier, *A Communications Theory of Urban Growth* (Cambridge: M.I.T. Press, 1962), also abound.

[12] Besides offices held, positional notions of role may look to similarities in behavior patterns or in reactions by significant others. See Bruce J. Biddle and Edwin J. Thomas, eds., *Role Theory* (New York: Wiley, 1966), ch. 2. C. Wright Mills, *The Power Elite* (New York: Oxford University Press, 1956) employs the office-role approach extensively, but the method need not eventuate in monist findings. Compare, for example, Robert O. Tilman, *Bureaucratic Transition in Malaya* (Durham: Duke University Press, 1964) or the historical chapters in Robert A. Dahl, *Who Governs?* (New Haven: Yale University Press, 1961).

does not mean a new pattern of communication, for saliency inheres in role relationships and not in particular occupants of roles.

Third, our idea of permeability accords well with concepts employed in both small group studies and macroscopic political analyses. Goffman, for example, utilizes dramaturgical language such as regions, audiences, and performances in explaining the dynamics of interpersonal behavior, while Agger and Schattschneider examine participatory scope and bias at urban and national political levels. All three theorists, in short, concentrate upon fluctuations in numbers and kinds of actors, fluctuations that derive from changes in the filtering rates of boundary membranes.[13]

Though lines can be drawn from all seven of the interaction aspects we record to significant theories in the social sciences, we shall concentrate here on only one other attribute, namely, the specification of temporal position by quartile, since it may appear to readers least precedented and most in need of justification. Dividing narratives into time periods is, of course, not particularly novel. Students of community decision-making who do this, however, ordinarily use substantive criteria. They may employ simple rubrics like initiation of action, fixing priorities or allocating preferred values, legitimization, and implementation,[14] or they may propound quite rich and complex phase theories.[15] Whether spare or elaborate, all such models are beset by serious problems. This is especially true when stages appear to be telescoped, eliminated, repeated, or taken out of order, or when cycles are repeated in whole or in part.

Although the myriad difficulties of substantive-phase analysis are avoided in such non-temporal approaches as transactional and value-added logic,[16] the gains involve rather serious costs. After all, events do occur through time, and their order is scarcely a trivial consideration. A better solution would see temporal units retained but not tied to any substantive determinism. The technique of quartile mapping fits these goals, since it permits the interaction flow in each narrative to be divided consistently into four periods of equal duration. The procedure may

[13] Erving Goffman, *The Presentation of Self in Everyday Life* (Garden City, N.Y.: Doubleday, 1959), E. E. Schattschneider, *The Semisovereign People* (New York: Holt, Rinehart and Winston, 1960), and Robert E. Agger, Daniel Goldrich, and Bert E. Swanson, *The Rulers and the Ruled* (New York: Wiley, 1964), chs. 1, 2, 3, and 14.

[14] The example is from M. Kent Jennings, *Community Influentials* (New York: Free Press, 1964), pp. 107–8. Compare Irwin T. Sanders, "The Stages of a Community Controversy," *Journal of Social Issues,* 17 (1961), 55–66.

[15] See especially James S. Coleman, *Community Conflict* (Glencoe: Free Press, 1957).

[16] For the former, see footnote 11 in this chapter. Neil J. Smelser, *Theory of Collective Behavior* (New York: Free Press, 1963) exemplifies the latter.

initially seem like arbitrary butchering, since no attempt is made to carve at joints, but activities in society do not really come jointed anyway.[17] Furthermore, even if optimal boundaries could be devised for one case study, identical limits would surely not be best for most others.

While our method of temporal analysis is unfamiliar in studies of community decision-making, it does resemble a device used by students of small groups. For example, Bales makes time the sole criterion of phase in interaction processes.[18] Furthermore, the same criterion is implicit in Wheaton's recent paper on the urban decision process. In particular, his chart delineating the "flow of communication in a developmental decision process" appears graphically to assume three time periods of equal length.[19] Quartile determination, in other words, like role or permeability, does link with and acquire relevance from broader theoretical considerations in adjacent studies.

Two concluding observations should be made before we turn to the comparative data that our methods have uncovered. First, our conceptual framework is obviously not as complex or sophisticated as the theoretical store on which it draws. Role theory, for example, concerns far more than the positional attribute we have coded; yet we say nothing about role sets, role performance, role conflict, and all the other complexities of this fascinating, and bewildering, field. Similarly, the wonderful and ingenious communications models developed by Gore and by Deutsch far exceed our simple analytic devices. Data restrictions argue for our having "trimmed our sails," but the spareness of our categories should not be overlooked, even though hopefully they still accord in spirit and general outline with the theories cited.

Second, and more positively, we are using the detail and verisimilitude of case studies not as cues for speculation but as the stuff in which

[17] There is, of course, a considerable body of quite venerable opinion to the contrary. Indeed, carving at joints was a major precept in Plato's later dialectic. Such an outlook, however, appears to us indemonstrable and flatly wrong.

[18] Phase division was accomplished, in fact, by applying a yardstick and a pair of shears to the paper tapes on which the conversations of groups had been coded. Bales's earlier phasing practices also had a largely temporal basis. The procedure employed was for "the total period [to be] divided so that each phase includes one-third of the acts of the total set. (This is approximately equal to a time division into thirds, though not quite, since we have observed that there is some tendency for the interaction to speed up toward the latter part of topical cycles.)" See Robert F. Bales and Fred L. Strodtbeck, "Phases in Group Problem-Solving," *Journal of Abnormal and Social Psychology,* 46 (1951), 484–95.

[19] William L. C. Wheaton, "Integration at the Urban Level: Political Influence and the Decision Process," in Philip E. Jacob and James V. Toscano, eds., *The Integration of Political Communities* (Philadelphia: Lippincott, 1964), pp. 120–42 and especially p. 130.

interesting constellations of phenomena are firmly grounded.[20] Perhaps an analogy from an adjacent branch of inquiry may clarify the distinction. It is one thing to select totals from public opinion polls in order to illustrate a thesis that has been otherwise derived. It is something quite different to undertake an internal analysis of polls in order to find interesting patterns that the data themselves form.[21] In the following discussion, we try to approximate the latter type of procedure.

[20] See Chapter I of this volume.

[21] Contrast, for example, Gabriel A. Almond, *The American People and Foreign Policy* (New York: Harcourt, Brace, 1950), with Almond and Sidney Verba, *The Civic Culture* (Princeton: Princeton University Press, 1963), or with Robert R. Alford, *Party and Society* (Chicago: Rand McNally, 1963).

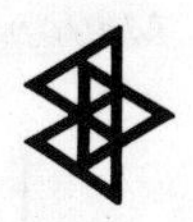

CHAPTER III

Contours of Interaction

THIS CHAPTER AND the next two set forth various analyses of the data. In all, some 3,310 interactions have been recorded, the range for the 32 cases extending from 37 to 287. With the first 10 and last 5 per cent of interactions eliminated from each narrative, a net total of 2,842 remains. Table III.1 lists the author, title, source, net interaction count, and time interval for the cases. It also stipulates abbreviated designations by which the cases will henceforth be called.

Unless otherwise indicated, tables here and in Chapter IV are based on all 32 cases.[1] Obviously, this does not constitute a random compilation, for published cases hardly sample all metropolitan decision-making randomly. Furthermore, our selection within the available case literature proceeds from certain substantive and methodological criteria and not from statistical considerations.

These criteria help explain the omission of several well-known studies. Cases are included only if their starting date, i.e., the date of the first interaction in the first quartile, does not precede America's entry into World War II: this eliminates the two metropolitan cases in the Stein collection.[2] Book length investigations[3] are excluded, though easily

[1] The analyses of cities in the first half of Chapter V also utilize four cases from Beloit, Wisconsin, and five from Oberlin, Ohio. Full information about these nine cases is found in Table IV.1.

[2] Herbert Kaufman, "Gotham in the Air Age," in Harold Stein, ed., *Public Administration and Policy Development* (New York: Harcourt, Brace, 1952), pp. 143–97, and Frank C. Abbot, "The Cambridge City Manager," *ibid.*, pp. 573–620.

[3] For example, Harold Kaplan, *Urban Renewal Politics* (New York: Columbia University Press, 1963), or Martin Meyerson and Edward C. Banfield, *Politics, Planning, and the Public Interest* (New York: Free Press, 1964).

TABLE III.1

Metropolitan Cases Used in Interaction Analysis

Author	*Title*	*Source (See key below)*	*Net Inter-action Count*	*Time Span (Yr.)*	*Time Span (Mo.)*	*Abbreviated Designation*
Altshuler	The Ancker Hospital Site Controversy	*City Planning,* 144–88	81	5	1	Altshuler-Hospital
Banfield	The Exhibition Hall	*Political Influence,* 190–231	85	6		Banfield-Hall
Banfield	The Fort Dearborn Project	*Political Influence,* 126–58	44	4	4	Banfield-Project
Birkhead	The Post-War Report	*Syracuse,* 47–74	68	3		Birkhead-Report
Crain	Baltimore	*School Desegregation,* 93–103	31	1		Crain-Baltimore
Crain	Buffalo	*School Desegregation,* 75–91	37	4	3	Crain-Buffalo
Crain	St. Louis	*School Desegregation,* 13–31	51	3		Crain-St. Louis
Crain	San Francisco	*School Desegregation,* 105–24	52	2	7	Crain-San Francisco
Crain and Inger	New Orleans—The Failure of an Elite	*New Orleans,* 15–87	210	6	6	Crain-New Orleans
Davies	Seaside-Hammels	*Groups and Renewal,* 30–71	163	8	1	Davies-Rockaway
Davies	The West Village	*Groups and Renewal,* 72–109	122	1	11	Davies-Village
Davies	The West Side Urban Renewal Area	*Groups and Renewal,* 110–46	89	6	1	Davies-West Side
Gladfelter	Jets for the Great Swamp?	Frost, 302–18	58		2	Gladfelter-Airport
Gladfelter	Water for Wauwatosa	Frost, 280–91	35	4	8	Gladfelter-Water
Herman	The Metropolitan Sewage Treatment Plant	*Syracuse,* 80–110	89	7	8	Herman-Sewage
Keeley	Moses on the Green	Bock, 25–34	47		3½	Keeley-Moses
Logue and Bock	The Demotion of Deputy Chief Inspector Goldberg	Bock, 229–62	67		10	Logue-Demotion
Mann and Stout	The Broome County Airport	Frost, 321–36	62	3	2	Mann-Airport
Martin	Water for the Suburbs	*Syracuse,* 111–30	69	11	11	Martin-Water
Mowitz and Wright	Detroit's Metropolitan Airport	*Metropolis,* 295–401	244	12	1	Mowitz-Airport
Mowitz and Wright	Detroit's City-County Building	*Metropolis,* 141–68	80	6	11	Mowitz-Building

Mowitz and Wright	The Urban Renewal of Corktown	*Metropolis,* 81–139	139	12	6	Mowitz-Corktown
Mowitz and Wright	The Extension of the Lodge Expressway	*Metropolis,* 403–63	100	1	4	Mowitz-Expressway
Mowitz and Wright	The Gratiot Redevelopment Project	*Metropolis,* 11–79	149	7	4	Mowitz-Gratiot
Mowitz and Wright	The Case of the Missing Port	*Metropolis,* 235–94	142	5	3	Mowitz-Port
Mowitz and Wright	Water for Southwestern Wayne County	*Metropolis,* 169–234	95	4	7	Mowitz-Water
Muir	Defending "The Hill" Against Metal Houses	Bock, 3–24	107		5½	Muir-Houses
Peabody	Seattle Seeks a Tax	Bock, 493–514	73	1	3	Peabody-Tax
Pomper	The New York Fluoridation Dispute	Frost, 50–61	33	8	6	Pomper-Fluoridation
Rossi and Dentler	South West Hyde Park	*Politics of Renewal,* 156–90	71	1		Rossi-Hyde Park
Sherwood and Markey	The Mayor and the Fire Chief	Bock, 109–134	104	1	11	Sherwood-Chief
Simon	The New York Hospitals Controversy	Frost, 255–64	45	1	6	Simon-Hospitals

Key for Sources

Bock — Edwin A. Bock, ed., *State and Local Government* (University, Alabama: University of Alabama Press, 1963).

City Planning — Alan A. Altshuler, *The City Planning Process* (Ithaca: Cornell University Press, 1965).

Frost — Richard T. Frost, ed., *Cases in State and Local Government* (Englewood Cliffs, N.J.: Prentice-Hall, 1961).

Groups and Renewal — J. Clarence Davies III, *Neighborhood Groups and Urban Renewal* (New York: Columbia University Press, 1966).

Metropolis — Robert J. Mowitz and Deil S. Wright, *Profile of a Metropolis* (Detroit, Wayne State University Press, 1962).

New Orleans — Robert L. Crain and Morton Inger, *School Desegregation in New Orleans* (Chicago: National Opinion Research Center, 1966).

Political Influence — Edward C. Banfield, *Political Influence* (New York: Free Press, 1961).

Politics of Renewal — Peter H. Rossi and Robert A. Dentler, *The Politics of Urban Renewal* (New York: Free Press, 1961).

School Desegregation — Robert L. Crain, *School Desegregation in the North* (Chicago: National Opinion Research Center, 1966).

Syracuse — Roscoe C. Martin, Frank J. Munger, *et al., Decisions in Syracuse* (Bloomington: Indiana University Press, 1961).

detached narratives that comprise chapters in books, e.g., Rossi and Dentler's treatment of South West Hyde Park, are retained. Cases are also omitted if their interactions are too few[4] or largely undatable,[5] if their content is mainly non-metropolitan,[6] if they fictionalize[7] or analytically distill[8] interaction data, or if their subject matter focuses on either electoral and intraparty campaigning[9] or subjective states of mind among decision-makers.[10] These omissions are intended to increase intercase comparability by eliminating cases that are exceptionally old, extraordinarily detailed, non-metropolitan, or electoral; and to facilitate the assemblage of factual, explicit, objective, specific, datable interactions amenable to our code procedures.

Though many cases have been omitted, some quite excellent by other standards, a large and varied group of studies remains. Most of them are by authors well known in the genre or from collections familiar to political scientists and sociologists. Except for Crain's five accounts of school desegregation controversies, the source material is easily available in regularly published formats.[11] Readers thus may go back to *our* original data, in a way neither we nor they can to the original data of the primary investigators, and see if they would achieve similar results from our methods. In addition, a careful reexamination of the case studies should

[4] In general, "too few" has been defined as less than 30 within the four quartiles. This restriction necessitates the omission of such brief cases as the five about real estate development in Roscoe C. Martin, Frank J. Munger, *et al., Decisions in Syracuse* (Bloomington: Indiana University Press, 1961), pp. 240–61.

[5] A paucity of dates excludes Banfield's otherwise excellent study "The Branch Hospital." See Edward C. Banfield, *Political Influence* (New York: Free Press, 1961), pp. 15–56.

[6] Cases are deemed non-metropolitan either (1) because their activities are too narrow in scope to indicate truly city-wide or area-wide importance, or (2) because they occur mainly outside the metropolitan area, usually at the state capitol. Mariana Robinson, "The Coming of Age of the Langley Porter Clinic," in Frederick C. Mosher, ed., *Governmental Reorganizations* (Indianapolis: Bobbs-Merrill, 1967), 251–300, exemplifies the first sort of exclusion, while three of Banfield's cases ("The Welfare Merger," "The Chicago Transit Authority," and "The Chicago Campus," *op. cit.*, pp. 57–125 and 159–89), or William J. Gore and Evelyn Shipman, "Commuters vs. the Black Ball Line," in Edwin A. Bock, ed., *State and Local Government* (University, Ala.: University of Alabama Press, 1963), pp. 69–105, reflect the latter consideration.

[7] For example, there are studies of "Lawndale" and of "Bay City" in Robert L. Crain, *School Desegregation in the North* (Chicago: National Opinion Research Center, 1966), pp. 33–63.

[8] See especially Robert A. Dahl, *Who Governs?* (New Haven: Yale University Press, 1961), pp. 115–62.

[9] Thus, most of the Eagleton Institute studies.

[10] Most notable among this sort of case are the two accounts of city plans and planners in Alan A. Altshuler, *The City Planning Process* (Ithaca: Cornell University Press, 1965), pp. 84–143 and 189–296.

[11] Crain's cases, which we examined in mimeograph, are now available in *The Politics of School Desegregation* (Chicago: Aldine, 1968).

facilitate improvements in both rationales and detailed procedures of analysis.

Besides indicating the range of available cases, our sample also possesses its own intrinsic worth. It relates issues and decisions that emerged within many of this nation's largest cities—New York City, Chicago, and Detroit are particularly well-represented—and that attracted considerable public interest. Although these studies scarcely provide a key for all decision processes, their content is surely not wholly misleading or atypical. Most case collections, whether by city, issue, or some more abstract criteria, contain what their authors and editors deem a fair sample of topics. Moreover, by basing our general findings not on one or two cases but on a large group, we reduce further the likelihood of having fastened on wholly anomalous events.

The analyses in the present chapter are macroscopic, affording an overview of decision processes within and across case studies. The basic analytic unit employed is the distribution of interactions (meetings, messages, and public statements) and interaction aspects (actors, locale, permeability, formality, and continuity) within quartiles. Percentages are computed separately for each case, and the cases are weighted equally. The tables presented below are based on measures of central tendencies among the 32 studies.[12]

Before examining these patterns, however, it might be well first to consider the time spans of the narratives. As Table III.1 indicates, the four quartiles of Gladfelter-Airport and Keeley-Moses consume only two months and three-and-one-half months, respectively. In contrast, Mowitz-Airport and Mowitz-Corktown each last more than a dozen years. Most of our cases, however, fall well between these extremes, with the median somewhat above four years. Indeed, one might assert that there are "natural limits" to the longevity of most decision processes in metropolitan case studies, for critical and controversial issues seldom reach prompt resolution, while struggles that continue indefinitely seem to lie outside the ambit of single cases. At the least, one conclusion is incontestable from the chronology in Table III.1: processes of the kinds encompassed by our sample have life expectancies in years, not weeks.

Our chief interest, of course, is not in the durability of issue controversies but in the identification of temporal features *within* them. In particular, our emphasis has been on tracing changes in interaction intensity through time. By the application of quartile divisions to narratives,[13] one can investigate, for example, whether cases gradually "heat up," exhibit-

[12] In Chapters IV and V the analyses are more microscopic, the basic analytic unit is the interaction (and its aspects), and frequencies are computed across cases so that weighting occurs in proportion to the case detail.
[13] Quartile analysis is discussed at length in Chapter II.

ing over time increased communication between key actors, or whether public issues typically reveal flurries of activity during more nascent periods. Such patterns may be clearer for particular issues, actors, or settings, but they are also discernible for communications in general.

Our expectation was that the rate of interpersonal communication would intensify through time. Presumably controversies gain momentum as larger numbers of individuals and groups discover their stake in the outcome, assemble their resources, and act to influence critical decisions. The data are consonant with these assumptions, although the increase in interactions is not smooth. For the 32 cases the average percentage of coded interactions in the first quartile is 19, with successive periods containing 22, 24, and 35 per cent. If for each case the quartiles with the highest and the lowest frequency of communication are recorded, a similar, if sharper, picture emerges. As Table III.2 shows, the first quartile commonly has the smallest rate of interaction, and the fourth quartile about as often has the largest.[14]

TABLE III.2

Interaction Rates Usually Increase over Time

Quartile		*Percentage* *Highest in Interactions*	*Percentage* *Lowest in Interactions*
1		16	41
2		21	28
3		21	16
4		42	15
	% =	100	100
	N =	33*	32

* In one case an equal number of interactions appears in two quartiles.

Despite obvious trends, Table III.2 also implies considerable variation among the cases. Five of them—some 16 per cent—reach an interaction peak in the first quartile, while in a like number of narratives—not all the same—interaction is least frequent in the fourth quartile. For example, a controversy in New York City (Keeley-Moses), stemming from the decision of Park Commissioner Robert Moses to blacktop a portion of Central Park, induced a stream of communications in the first quartiles that was not matched later. Similar distributions occur during Seattle's

[14] This finding may result from case authors' tendency to arrive on the scene of issue controversies during later stages. However, the diversity in rates from case to case (described immediately below in the text) makes such a research bias unlikely as a total or even prime explanation. Also see notes 17 and 31 in this chapter.

search for additional tax revenues (Peabody-Tax) and during the formulation and debate of Syracuse's postwar planning report (Birkhead-Report).[15]

Another aspect of case diversity is in the range of interactions across quartiles. Some issues may exhibit a fairly steady stream of communications, others a noticeable ebb and flow, and yet others wide swings over time. One simple way to measure such variability within cases is to calculate average deviations from a uniform 25 per cent distribution of interactions in each quartile. As Table III.3 indicates, these deviations range from 3.5 to 30.0 per cent, with roughly a third of the cases below 10 per cent, between 10 and 20 per cent, and above 20 per cent.

In narratives with but slight variability, issues arise and ultimately recede from public attention, with the communicative activity that intervenes proceeding in a steady flow. Urban renewal cases in Detroit and New York City, a projected commercial-residential-civic improvement in Chicago, and the adjustment of water resources between Syracuse and its suburbs exemplify issues with relatively flat process rates. Yet even the Detroit renewal case (Mowitz-Gratiot) exhibits some unevenness. Interactions declined somewhat during its third quartile—about two years—while the city was seeking private developers and while city-appointed architects were objecting to the plans proposed. In contrast, activity rose above average during the fourth quartile when the project was rescued from collapse and a citizens committee worked vigorously to refine the objectives of renewal and renovate its administration.

Cases with large deviations include the school integration controversies of Crain-San Francisco and Crain-New Orleans. In the San Francisco narrative, more than three-quarters of all interactions cluster in a single quartile. A series of critical determinations by school officials occurred early in the case, while related interactions diminished rapidly over the course of a year. In New Orleans, school desegregation was a low-keyed process for more than seven years—until the school board was forced to put a plan into operation. Nearly 90 per cent of the communications fall in the last quartile, when turbulent local and state protest activity flared up. Skewing similar to that in New Orleans accounts for the high deviation scores of two New York City cases, Logue-Demotion and Simon-

[15] Variability is perhaps most evident when interaction frequencies in each case are ordered by all four quartiles. Some 24 different rankings are theoretically possible, and the 32 cases exhibit no fewer than 19 of them. Indeed, only three cases precisely follow a progression of increasing communications behavior from beginning to end. Nonetheless, the larger pattern is still evident, for 20 of the cases contain only a single "error" or deviation from a simple 1, 2, 3, 4 quartile ordering. Furthermore, except for four studies, all narratives have more frequent interactions after their temporal midpoint.

TABLE III.3

Cases Vary Widely in Their Average Deviations from Uniform Temporal Distributions

Case	*Average Deviation from Uniform 25% Distribution*
Mowitz-Gratiot	3.5
Martin-Water	4.5
Banfield-Project	4.5
Davies-Rockaway	4.5
Pomper-Fluoridation	6.3
Mowitz-Airport	6.5
Gladfelter-Airport	6.7
Mowitz-Port	7.0
Mowitz-Building	7.0
Rossi-Hyde Park	8.7
Crain-Baltimore	10.7
Davies-West Side	11.0
Gladfelter-Water	12.0
Mowitz-Water	12.0
Mowitz-Expressway	12.5
Mowitz-Corktown	13.0
Sherwood-Chief	14.0
Herman-Sewage	15.0
Davies-Village	15.5
Mann-Airport	15.7
Banfield-Hall	16.0
Muir-Houses	17.7
Crain-Buffalo	21.0
Birkhead-Report	21.5
Peabody-Tax	22.5
Crain-St. Louis	23.0
Altshuler-Hospital	24.3
Keeley-Moses	25.0
Crain-San Francisco	26.0
Crain-New Orleans	27.5
Logue-Demotion	27.7
Simon-Hospitals	30.0

The signs of the individual deviations are omitted in these calculations, the formula being $AD = \frac{\Sigma|X-\overline{X}|}{4}$.

Hospitals. A crackdown on social and charitable gambling, which resulted in the demotion of a high-ranking police officer, and the efforts of city health officials to avoid a stand on birth control were both characterized by sharp upswings in activity during the fourth quartile. The controversies had remained dormant for a long time until single events—a letter of complaint to the police department, a statement of policy by a hospital commissioner—spurred bureaucratic and community reactions.

These numerical findings, and the examples they include, suggest that the time dimension provides a valuable perspective for understanding decision processes. Admittedly, focusing solely on broad temporal outlines obscures as well as reveals. Such analysis, however, does give notice of the enormous diversity in case studies. The patterns delineated in the narratives conform to widely different temporal shapes; there is clearly no single index to the life and death of issue controversies. Indeed, we have no right to expect one.

MODES OF INTERACTION

To assume that interactions bind decision-making processes scarcely describes the substance of these ties. What modes of communication do case actors in fact employ as they negotiate, criticize, collaborate, and advise? Table III.4 shows that interactions tend to be indirect rather than face-to-face. The mean distribution for messages and public statements together in the 32 cases is 60 per cent. From case to case, in other words, three interactions out of five occur through letters, over the telephone, in reports and memoranda, or via such impersonal media as newspapers and television. The remaining interactions involve direct encounters, some by small groups and others at public gatherings.

TABLE III.4
Messages and Public Statements Are Together More Prevalent than Meetings in Every Time Period

	Mean of Interaction Percentages in Quartile				
Mode	*1*	*2*	*3*	*4*	*in All Quartiles*
Meetings	46	38	33	42	40
Messages	35	42	43	32	36
Public statements	19	20	24	26	24

Unless otherwise indicated, all tables in this chapter have *columns* totalling 100 per cent.

Although detailed comparisons of behavior by mode will not be made here,[16] Table III.4 does draw attention to the frequent incidence of public statements. In the main, the press serves as an intermediary for these communications. Many remarks by public officials find their way into the mass media, and often the strategies of amplification are calculated well in advance. In addition, private individuals and organizations may deliberately use the press to communicate with others in the formulating and influencing of metropolitan policies. Thus, in Herman-Sewage

[16] Much of Chapter IV is devoted to this type of analysis.

the Syracuse city engineer made known his opposition to a proposed plan by providing the press with the text of a letter he wrote to the mayor. Similarly, in a New York City urban renewal case, Davies-West Side, a Puerto Rican housing committee fed information regularly to the city's two Spanish-language newspapers. Nor is the press itself only a neutral medium. In Altshuler-Hospital, for example, the St. Paul newspapers played a vigorous role in the controversy over the location of a new county medical facility.

Although the mean of interaction percentages coded as public statements is just under one-quarter, individual cases differ over a wide range. In Mowitz-Building and Mann-Airport, less than 10 per cent of the interactions are public statements. For eleven other cases, including five of the seven from New York City, the figures are 30 per cent or more. Indeed, in Gladfelter-Airport, which describes a broadly based attack on the Port Authority's plan for a new airport in suburban New Jersey, more than half the interactions are conveyed through the news media.[17]

The quartile data in Table III.4 do not reveal any overwhelming temporal trends, but some of the individual figures are suggestive. For example, the middle periods, and especially quartile three, contain smaller proportions of face-to-face interactions. One possible and interesting implication is that direct sessions among case actors may be most valuable in the initial and the final stages of community decision-making.

INTERACTION PARTICIPANTS

Anyone concerned with the basic components of decision processes must inquire about the persons who interact. To be sure, participation is not an infallible indicator of influence, but often there does appear to be a strong association. The general finding in small group research, that interaction is unevenly distributed and that persons of high status and power initiate and receive more direct communications,[18] should perhaps be applied to large-scale metropolitan settings with some caution. But the converse proposition, that individuals and groups that rarely interact will have little influence over decisions, does seem defensible. Indeed, it would hold

[17] It is plausible that issue controversies receiving extensive coverage in the news media differ from those with less public visibility. Admittedly, findings may occasionally be mere artifacts of the information available to case writers. Newspaper stories are highly accessible, and extensive reliance on them may indicate a poorly researched narrative. The figure of 24 per cent in Table III.4, however, hardly seems excessive. For city-by-city discussions also see Chapter V.

[18] See Barry E. Collins and Harold Guetzkow, *A Social Psychology of Group Processes for Decision-Making* (New York: Wiley, 1964), pp. 172 and 187.

true no matter whether the metropolis itself were monolithic or polyarchic in its influence structure.[19]

The data show that many interests, including various levels of government, both openly and *in camera* attempt to shape the substance of public decisions. While any ranking of actors[20] by degree of participation, as in Table III.5, reflects idiosyncracies in the case studies sampled, the breadth of issues in our selection should obviate serious bias. For the same reason most of the actor categories employed should arouse little surprise. Occasionally, though, the repetition of certain types of controversies will cause particular groups to loom large in the total figures and to warrant special encoding. Thus, our inclusion of several cases dealing with school integration has obliged us to record school officials separately from others in local government.

TABLE III.5

Rank Ordering of Actor Participants Indicates Some Anticipated Levels of Activity

Rank	Actor	Rank	Actor
1	Appointed city	13	Court
2	Elected city	14	Religion
3	Business	15	Local intergovernmental
4	*Ad hoc*	16	Governmentally appointed planning and sounding board
5	Professional		
6.5	State	17	Elected county
6.5	School	18	Elected suburban
8	Civic	19	Party functionary
9	Appointed county	20.5	Other interest group
10	Communications	20.5	Other governmental
11	Civil rights	22	Appointed suburban
12	Federal	23	Labor

Ranks were determined case by case according to the proportion that each category's interactions were of all interactions. Figures in this table are the mean of these ranks over the 32 cases. The categories "non-affiliated" and "unspecified" are omitted here. For further information on them see Table IV.5.

Since most of the narratives in our sample concern authoritative decisions, it is not surprising that appointed and elected officials of local

[19] In the former type of community, significant and frequent interactions might not be so evident on the surface, but it is doubtful that they lie deeply buried. Hunter does not appear to have probed further in Atlanta than Dahl in New Haven in order to ferret out crucial interaction data. See Floyd Hunter, *Community Power Structure* (Chapel Hill: University of North Carolina Press, 1953). Moreover, it is the supposed ability of the power attribution method *readily* to identify important kinds of influence, even in communities a researcher does not know well, that has lent this approach its measure of popularity. If anything, writers in the Inter-University Case Program tradition often put more effort into going "behind the scenes."

[20] The term "actors," here and elsewhere in this study, refers not to given individuals but to role categories. The complete actor code is listed in the Appendix.

government occupy the first ranks in Table III.5. It was also to be expected that businessmen would be strongly involved in urban decision-making, for even vigorous skeptics of economic-dominants theories recognize considerable activity by business in public issue controversies. Whether united or not, business here is clearly preeminent among the non-governmental categories. The well-known capacity of urban dwellers to organize against apparent threats to their interests is also born out by the high ranking of *ad hoc* groups. Organizations like the West Side Tenants Committee, the Jetport Action Association, and the Citizens' Committee Against Proposition Five sprang up rapidly and often dominated events. Only the frequent interactions of professional personnel—mainly architects and engineers—might have been unpredicted. Our sample of issue controversies evidently furnished a large opportunity for specialists, particularly those with the appearance of disinterestedness. For complex determinations, like building expressways and sewage treatment facilities, individuals or firms with expertise were indispensable allies to other actors.

The relatively pronounced position of appointed county officials in Table III.5 is a natural consequence of a case sample laden with area-wide issues. Decisions about highway access routes, port facility improvements, and civic center construction, to name but a few, necessitated the participation of county bureaucracies that share responsibilities with city authorities, e.g., Detroit's Wayne County, Syracuse's Onondaga County, and Chicago's Cook County. A wide spill-over of local problems is evidenced by the still greater activity of state personnel, who served as advocates and mediators in controversies over water resources, fluoridation, and school integration. The intervention of federal actors, although less prominent by the accounting measures in Table III.5, is particularly manifest for urban renewal and airport construction, both being good illustrations of direct federal involvement in urban affairs.

Among the least prominent actor categories, two deserve special notice. The data plainly confirm the common impression that neither political parties nor organized labor participates frequently in community controversies. Among the 23 categories, party functionaries place nineteenth and labor officials twenty-third. Minor exceptions include Gladfelter-Airport, where the prospect of additional jobs gave labor an incentive to speak up, and Herman-Sewage, where Democratic party leaders interpreted the proposed metropolitan sanitation plan as an attempted "power grab" by area Republicans.

It would be interesting to know whether or not this participation by actors exhibits any clearly temporal features. Do some categories show relatively steady interaction rates? Do others play especially active roles during the incipient stage of a controversy or perhaps only after it has matured? A partial answer to these inquiries is provided by Table III.6. The tendency for the interventions of all actor categories to become more concentrated over time is consonant, of course, with the general rates of communications in the four quartiles.[21] Equally noticeable, however, is actor variability. Indeed, at least five patterns of distribution can be elicited from Table III.6. First, there is a gradual increase in participation rates through time, achieved by appointed and elected city officials and also by state and appointed county officials. A second pattern, exemplified by the business and professional categories, shows a slower rise from quartiles one to two, but a much sharper change in rates through quartiles three and four. Another tendency, that of a continually steep increase across quartiles, characterizes civic groups as well as federal, intergovernmental, and religious actor categories. *Ad hoc* groups, civil rights actors, and school officials reveal a fourth pattern, with appreciable drops in their participation rates in the second quartile interrupting what other-

TABLE III.6
Actor Participation Rates over Time Follow Several Distinctive Patterns

	Mean of Interaction Percentages in Quartile				
Actor Category	*1*	*2*	*3*	*4*	*Number of Cases*
Appointed city	18	26	27	29	18
Elected city	17	25	26	32	20
Business	19	19	26	36	15
Ad hoc	19	10	31	40	11
Professional	15	18	28	39	11
State	21	29	21	29	7
School	18	9	25	48	6
Civic	7	24	31	38	6
Appointed county	22	24	19	35	7
Communications	13	19	13	55	5
Civil rights	28	13	25	34	4
Federal	13	16	25	46	6
Religion	5	8	39	48	5
Local intergovernmental	7	15	38	40	4

Only those cases in which an actor category evidences at least ten coded interactions are included. Categories that satisfy this minimum in fewer than four cases are omitted. *Rows* total 100 per cent.

[21] For the most part, rates of participation increase as one proceeds from quartile one to quartile four. Furthermore, no actor has a higher average distribution before the temporal midpoint than after it.

wise is a clear trend toward increased participation. Finally, as the communications (mass media) category shows, there can be a pattern that is characterized more than anything else by an extremely heavy concentration of interactions in the final quartile.

Though interpretations must be made cautiously, especially where the number of cases is small, certain conclusions seem warranted from Table III.6. Government actors generally exhibit a fairly continuous role in issue controversies.[22] Their increases in participation over time are not large. Interaction by appointed and elected city officials is particularly uniform across quartiles, a fact that accords with these categories' being at the nucleus of many metropolitan decision processes. Business and professional groups also play a fairly comprehensive part in our sample of narratives. The sharper increases over time for civic, religious, federal, and intergovernmental actors is consonant with the fact that these classifications are of relatively minor influence during the initial developments of a case. The pattern of communications exhibited by civil rights and *ad hoc* groups and by school officials indicates that however much they contribute toward setting the course for issues controversies, they often fail to sustain their activities during the second, and often crucial, period of decision-making. As for the communications industry (mainly the press), its editorial voice, although not entirely mute during the formative stages of issues, becomes far more audible after the lines of controversy have already been drawn.

A simple device for assigning temporal participation scores to actors consists of treating the quartiles as four points in time and computing a measure of central tendency. Thus, an actor category whose communications fall exclusively in the first quartile would score 1.00, while an index of 4.00 would be attained if its interactions all occur in the last quartile. Table III.7 lists temporal participation scores for 14 of the most frequent actor classifications in our data.

These scores permit a readily understandable summary of the average time of participation by various actors. *Ad hoc* and civil rights groups, for example, can be perceived as the earliest non-governmental actors. Federal and intergovernmental officials are clearly distinguishable from the other government categories, all of which communicate earlier in our cases. Business, though, demonstrates a fairly close temporal resemblance to government actors in the city and county.[23]

[22] Federal and intergovernmental actors, alluded to below, provide the chief exceptions.

[23] A more detailed and refined analysis of the temporal component in the behavior of non-governmental interests may be found in Tables IV.17 to IV.19.

TABLE III.7
Temporal Participation Scores Vary Among Actor Categories

Category	*Score*
State	2.58
Ad hoc	2.62
Appointed city	2.67
Appointed county	2.67
Civil rights	2.70
Elected city	2.73
Business	2.79
Professional	2.91
Civic	3.00
School	3.03
Federal	3.04
Communications	3.10
Local intergovernmental	3.11
Religion	3.30

Scores derive from the formula $\frac{1}{100}[\sum_{i=1}^{4}(qp)_i]$, where q is the quartile number and p the percentage of interactions in that quartile. This method of computation assumes a fairly linear distribution, an assumption that Table III.6 indicates is quite reasonable. The scores here are based on the data in Table III.6.

THE LOCALE OF INTERACTIONS

That modern conditions have greatly increased the impact of national influences on local politics and economics has long been recognized by students of the American scene.[24] The clear involvement of state and federal officials in our sample of cases also suggests that communication patterns will extend well beyond the boundaries of the core cities. Such inferences, though, do not specify how extensively extra-local channels are employed. For example, are sessions relevant to a metropolis frequently held outside that area? Does a tide of messages surge in from Washington and Wall Street? And do such locational aspects tend to vary during the time span of the narratives?

Some interactions, as Table III.8 indicates, do occur outside the metropolitan area, but the proportion of local communications is far more striking. If we confine ourselves to the loci of meetings and of the senders of messages, about nine in ten communications occur within local boundaries. The remaining one-tenth take place at roughly equal rates elsewhere

[24] For some early examples see Walter Lippmann, *The Phantom Public* (New York: Harcourt, Brace and World, 1925), part 3, and Robert S. Lynd and Helen M. Lynd, *Middletown in Transition* (New York: Harcourt, Brace, 1937).

in the state or beyond it. Table III.8 also clearly shows the absence of any temporal trend. Whether controversies are budding or mature, the city is the focus of communication activity.

TABLE III.8

Most Interactions Take Place in or near the Metropolitan Area

Locale	*Mean of Interaction Percentages in Quartile* 1	2	3	4	*in All Quartiles*
In or near the metropolitan area	92	89	89	90	89
Elsewhere in the state	5	7	5	5	6
Outside the state	3	3	5	4	4

Figures refer to the place of meetings or to the location of senders of messages and public statements. About 1 per cent of the interactions in each quartile were scored as indeterminate for locale. These are omitted from this table and account for the slight departures from column totals of 100 per cent.

This conclusion remains valid even under a closer examination of the two-way flows of communications. If one looks at the locations of sender-receiver pairs in messages,[25] results accrue that closely resemble those in Table III.8. Approximately 90 per cent of these messages involve initiators and receivers, both of whom are present in the metropolis; 6 per cent pass between the metropolitan area and the rest of the state; 4 per cent connect local persons with others outside the state; and only 1 per cent are among communicators totally beyond the city and its environs.

Thus, whatever the contribution to metropolitan decision-making of geographically distant private interests and government agencies, little evidence about it occurs in our sample of cases. The core city rather than its national setting provides the scene for most of the interactions described. This, of course, does not deny extra-local influence, for many state and federal offices maintain field representatives in large cities, while county bureaucracies, as well as industrial and professional interests, may also possess local bases of operation. Furthermore, actors need not be regularly located in the metropolis in order to press their demands there at meetings.

PERMEABILITY IN INTERACTIONS

Students of community politics have long been concerned with the permeability (or visibility) of decision-making. It has been traditionally held that for elites to be democratically accountable, general publics must

[25] Public statements are omitted, since their recipients—unspecified individuals—have no assignable location. For a detailed examination of this mode of interaction see Chapter IV.

be reasonably well aware of policy processes. Indeed, the extent to which interactions between actual decision-makers are visible has been treated as an index of the absence or presence of an elite power structure. The likelihood of tightly confined policy-making seems small where many individuals and groups seriously contest outcomes. This mobilization of public attention, which often facilitates groups seeking to improve their bargaining position, contrasts sharply with a process of hammering out decisions in private clubs and homes prior to their filtering down to underlings and eventually to the larger community.[26]

Although antithetical, these two views of metropolitan polities are not mutually exclusive. Even highly pluralistic formats can be studded with private or restricted interactions, while hierarchical decision structures may feel a need for public and publicized communications. By and large, though, the data in our sample fit better with the first viewpoint than with the second. As Table III.9 indicates, only about one interaction in five is impermeable, the other four all being partly or fully penetrated by larger publics. More than a third of the interactions, in fact, are exposed to quite wide audiences.

TABLE III.9

Partly Open Interactions Predominate in Every Time Period

Degree of Permeability	*Mean of Interaction in Quartile* 1	2	3	4	*Percentages in All Quartiles*
Impermeable	24	21	19	21	22
Partly permeable	44	48	46	40	42
Fully permeable	32	31	35	39	36

Partly permeable communications, the modal classification in all four quartiles of Table III.9, reflect ordinary institutional and situational limits rather than deliberate barriers to disclosure. For example:

> Tension once more gripped the small Fire Commission meeting room. A second vote was taken on the question, "Are firemen assigned on the basis of race alone?" "Yes," said the commission in a three to two vote, with Callanan, Yeamans, and Lollier in support and Rothmund and Joscelyn opposed.[27]

[26] The classic conflict is between Robert A. Dahl, *Who Governs?* (New Haven: Yale University Press, 1961), and Floyd Hunter, *Community Power Structure* (Chapel Hill: University of North Carolina Press, 1953). The two writers differ not only in their theoretical assertions but in the sorts of empirical evidence brought to their support.

[27] Sherwood-Chief, p. 123.

Or again, though here a message rather than a meeting:

> In November, 1946, following the passage of the Federal Airport Act, Mr. McFarland, the Planning Board Secretary, submitted an application for a "Class III airport," calling for an expenditure of $2,012,319 by Broome County and $1,967,319 by CAA, Washington.[28]

Or as one last illustration, this time primarily of an interest group meeting rather than a government session:

> On June 21, the night before the Board of Estimate's hearings on the final plan, the club [FDR-Woodrow Wilson Democrats] met. Attending the meeting as guests were Milton Mollen, the newly appointed Chairman of HRB, and Fried and Ratensky, also of HRB.[29]

Several hypotheses about the temporal placement of impermeable interactions seemed reasonable. For example, they might occur with particular frequency during the early stages of issue controversies. Before problems are fully apparent and many interests have recognized their stake in the issue, restrictive communications might well be quite common. Only over time would activities become more visible. An alternate and contrary supposition would be that impermeable interactions are most characteristic of the last stages of controversies. Only then, after much heat has been dissipated and the implications of the various options have become clear, do key participants settle down to confidential messages and hard bargaining sessions out of the view of larger publics.

Neither thesis nor others of this kind are supported by the data in Table III.9.[30] Impermeable interactions, to be sure, are more typical in the first quartile, and highly visible communications are more characteristic in the fourth. The differences, however, are slight. While there may be some temporal aspects to permeability—for example, by particular decision settings or issues—no patterns seem dominant enough to show through the gross data.

FORMALITY IN INTERACTIONS

One commonplace view of community decision-making, as we have mentioned earlier, is that it constitutes an essentially informal process. Individuals who matter are deemed able almost casually to predetermine courses of critical action. Off-the-record, in an atmosphere of congeniality and practicality—that is where the real choices are made. Questions like

[28] Mann-Airport, p. 327. (Seymour Z. Mann and Ronald M. Stout, "The Broome County Airport," in *Cases in State and Local Government,* Richard T. Frost, ed., © 1961, Prentice-Hall, Inc. By permission.)
[29] Davies-West Side, p. 138.
[30] Nor are they supported by the figures in Table IV.7.

the location of a public housing unit, the firing of a city manager, and the introduction of fluorine into a city's water supply are supposedly settled outside council halls. This conception of policy fits the elitist image of a small body of men who meet behind closed doors and effectively foreclose options, but it is also compatible with more polyarchic and competitive styles of politics. After all, much communication within and among groups is normally off-the-record and intimate.

TABLE III.10

Interactions Are Overwhelmingly Formal

Degree of Formality	*Mean of Interaction in Quartile* 1	2	3	4	*Percentages in All Quartiles*
Formal	85	83	87	82	83
Informal	15	17	13	18	17

The dominant note in our cases, though, is not one of informality but of a formal structuring in interactions. Table III.10 indicates in fact that on average more than four-fifths of all interactions could be characterized as formal, a proportion that remains fairly stable across quartiles. Our cases, in other words, furnish scant support for the proposition that metropolitan decisions are conspicuously informal in tone. Unrecorded telephone conversations, friendly briefings, and chance encounters are certainly not rare occurrences; but planned meetings with minutes taken, prepared releases to the press, and official letters are far more frequent.[31]

CONTINUITY IN INTERACTIONS

In addition to examining modes of communication, participants, locality, visibility, and formality, one can also describe the stability of relationships. Are cohesive interaction networks frequently evident in the case studies? If so, do they usually predate the particular issue controversy, or emerge only during that decision process? Furthermore, are there many interactions that seem unusual and unpatterned? Unquestionably, the prevalence of regular, case patterned, and ephemeral channels of communication varies with the issue concerned. The demotion of a police official, for all its controversy, is inherently more amenable to management within existing interaction patterns than is a decision over

[31] One might with reason object to these generalizations on the grounds that case authors are less likely to uncover off-the-record interactions than those more openly documented. Such omissions may, however, be largely compensated for by the authors' tendency to include and stress in their narratives those informal interactions of which they are cognizant.

the cross-city route for an expressway. But this aside, are any general propositions about communications networks in metropolitan decision-making suggested from our cases?

Large communities, like those that figure in our cases,[32] should be expected to employ regular decisional networks more frequently than case patterned or ephemeral ones. Confronted as they are by constant barrages of policy preferences, they necessarily develop and rely upon various institutionalized relationships in order to stabilize decision processes. These may be largely socio-economic, as elite theorists often assert, or may typically involve government and political officials, as pluralists usually testify. However this may be, the data in Table III.11 show that in general

TABLE III.11

Preestablished Interaction Networks Prevail in Every Time Period

Degree of Continuity	*Mean of Interaction in Quartile* 1	2	3	4	*Percentages in All Quartiles*
Regular	52	52	41	50	47
Case patterned	16	18	34	24	23
Ephemeral	32	30	25	26	30

about half the interactions in our cases occur within on-going interaction configurations. From Mann-Airport we have selected two illustrations of such established lines of communications, one inside government and one outside. Both reveal the capacity of old networks to handle new loads.

> After the meeting, County Attorney O'Brien checked with the New York Attorney-General on the requirement for a two-thirds majority in such a matter, and he was assured that the rule stood.
>
> Dr. Bowers and Dr. Moore were old friends, and while Dr. Moore was treating him [for an injured knee], he showed Dr. Bowers the letter from the CAA. Dr. Moore then raised the problem of how a unified proposal could be developed for presentation to the Board of Supervisors without the concurrent disrupting effect that public announcement of the CAA decision and conflict over a new airport could have before the proposal was submitted to the Supervisors.[33]

If case patterned and ephemeral interactions are aggregated, however, they comprise a majority of all interactions in the cases. Nearly a quarter of the communications follow pathways built during the life of the issues. Such new networks are frequently no less tightly bonded than

[32] For comparisons on continuity between large and small communities, see Chapter V.

[33] Mann-Airport, pp. 334 and 325.

those that predate the controversies. In addition, these case-patterned communications exhibit a strongly temporal character, comprising in the third quartile more than a third of all the interactions recorded. Here, for example, are two illustrations from Muir's case study in New Haven:

> During the meeting, one of the aldermen, Guida, had approached Grava with the suggestion that the [newly formed Hill Civic] Association seek the services of a lawyer named Joseph Koletsky.
>
> The next day when Mrs. Cook [of the League of Women Voters] heard from the discouraged Miss Grava [who resided in the threatened neighborhood] the outcome of the meeting, she was delighted that Koletsky had been obliging enough to quote a fee, and one that to her seemed so small.[34]

That some 30 per cent of all interactions should be outside *any* repetitive network is a good indicator of the plurality of interests engaging in these issue controversies. Such transient communications, by actors either incapable of more regularized relationships or lacking sufficient stakes for sustained participation, occur frequently throughout the course of the narratives. Thus, in Davies-Village, we read:

> On March 21 he [Borough President Dudley] spent an hour and a half inspecting the West Village and then submitted to an hour of questioning from neighborhood residents. He refused to concede that the city had erred in calling for urban renewal, although he stated that he was impressed by the high standards of the area.

Or, somewhat later:

> Eric Wensberg [of the Committee to Save West Village] spoke to Harry Van Arsdale, Jr., president of the Central Labor Council, and got him to over-rule the testimony that had been given CPC by the chairman of the Council's housing committee.[35]

The occurrence of such idiosyncratic interactions suggests rather pliant processes incompatible with a monolithic decision structure. In addition, the slightly higher concentration of unpatterned activity in early quartiles underlines the fact that these communications may come early enough to exert an impact upon the issue resolution.

THE EFFECTS OF CASE LENGTH

As we observed earlier in this chapter, case narratives vary considerably in length. Indeed, ten of the cases in our sample span at least a

[34] Muir-Houses, pp. 16–17.
[35] Davies-Village, pp. 93 and 106.

six-year period, while a similar number extend for less than two years. One might well inquire whether or not such differences in duration are associated with differences in the broad interaction features just reviewed.

One might suppose, for example, that the length of an issue controversy would affect interaction continuities. While regular channels that predate cases should show little or no change, case-patterned communications should be relatively more frequent in the lengthier cases and ephemeral communications somewhat less so.[36] Table III.12, which compares the ten longest and ten shortest cases, reveals the expected data relationships. Regular communications channels are employed at about the same rates in longer and shorter cases. Some 27 per cent of the interactions in the longer narratives are case patterned as against only 19 per cent in the briefer stories. Conversely, the shorter cases have more frequent incidences of ephemeral communications. Though modest, these differences do run in the predicted directions.

TABLE III.12

The Shortest and Longest Cases Show Different Distributions for Most Interaction Characteristics

Interaction Characteristic	*Mean of Interaction Percentages in Ten Shortest Cases*	*in Ten Longest Cases*
Mode		
Meetings	43	38
Messages and public statements	57	62
Permeability		
Impermeable	31	16
Partly permeable	32	53
Fully permeable	37	31
Formality		
Formal	74	89
Informal	26	11
Continuity		
Regular	50	48
Case patterned	19	27
Ephemeral	31	25

The ten shortest cases cover periods of from two months to one year, eleven months. The ten longest cases all last more than six years.

The differences in permeability and formality between the shorter and longer cases also deserve comment. As Table III.12 indicates, inter-

[36] This hypothesis is consonant with the finding in Table III.11 that case-patterned networks tend to develop relatively late in interaction processes.

actions in the narratives that span briefer periods are considerably more impermeable, somewhat more frequently intersected by large publics, and much more informal. Cases of shorter duration evidently are more intimate and more plastic as processes. This is reflected in *both* their impermeable (closed) and fully permeable (wide open) styles of communication. Indeed, as we have suggested earlier in this chapter, partly permeable interactions frequently reflect the nomal constraints that accompany formal institutions such as councils and commissions.

PROPOSITIONAL SUMMARY

The following generalizations about metropolitan decision processes can be elicited from the case data set forth in this chapter.

1. Issue controversies vary greatly in length, but usually have life spans of years rather than weeks or decades.
2. Although cases differ considerably in the constancy of their interaction rates over time, they typically exhibit increases as issues mature.
3. Interaction rates tend to be higher in the fourth than in any other quartile.
4. Indirect communication through messages and public statements occurs more frequently than direct communication through meetings; if the three modes are considered separately, however, face-to-face encounters are most prevalent.
5. Government officials from the central city are especially prominent actors in issue controversies, while business, *ad hoc,* and professional categories comprise the most overt non-government participants.
6. Among non-government interests, religion, political parties, and labor are particularly inactive in decision processes.
7. All actor categories show accelerated participation rates through time, despite considerable variation in the slope and regularity of the increase.
8. Participants differ markedly in relative time of intervention, with state and local government officials and such private interests as *ad hoc* groups, civil rights organizations, and business often entering cases quite early.
9. Interactions are overwhelmingly local in setting, a finding that applies not only to meetings but to origins and destinations of messages.
10. Throughout the time span of cases, interactions tend most often to be partly permeable and least often to be impermeable.

11. In each quartile more than four out of five interactions on average are formal in tone.
12. About one-half of all interactions occur within on-going communications networks.
13. While case-patterned interactions are more common in the two latter quartiles and ephemeral interactions are more characteristic of the first two, both of these continuity types are well represented throughout case processes.
14. Cases of short duration tend to be relatively intimate and plastic and contain noticeably higher percentages of impermeable, informal, and ephemeral interactions than do longer cases.

CHAPTER IV

Relationships Among Interaction Aspects

IN CONTRAST TO the synoptic approach of Chapter III, subsequent analyses are more microscopic. Discrete communications rather than case or quartile averages furnish the key analytic units. Frequencies are derived from individual interactions aggregated across all 32 case studies, with each interaction thereby having an equal weight.

Our focus will be not only on actor combinations, permeability, formality, and continuity but also on the way these interrelate in case processes. Separate sections are devoted to each characteristic, the general format being, first, to establish overall distributions by mode and quartile and, second, to assess the relation of the other attributes to these distributions. A final section of the chapter examines both intergovernmental communications and varieties of access between the government and selected non-government classifications. All these discussions are intended to supply a more complete inventory of interaction properties in metropolitan decision contexts.

CORRELATES OF ACTOR COMBINATIONS

Before actor categories are put into three broad groupings, it might be well to examine specific actor classifications in some detail. Table IV.1 rank orders the top 16 roles by the extent of their participation in meetings, messages, and public statements.[1] Many of the findings in this table

[1] These 16 include all roles that constitute 2 per cent or more of the total actor codes recorded. Furthermore, of the 9 categories omitted from this table, none ranks higher than 10 in any column and only one even exceeds 12.

TABLE IV.1

Some Actor Categories Exhibit Considerable Mode Specialization

Actor Category	*Rank Order by Meetings in Quartile*				*Rank Order by Messages in Quartile*				*Rank Order by Public Statements in Quartile*				*Summary Rank Order*[a]
	1	*2*	*3*	*4*	*1*	*2*	*3*	*4*	*1*	*2*	*3*	*4*	
Appointed city	1	2	1	1	1	1	1	1	4.5	3	2	5	1
Unspecified	5	10	10	6	6	10	7	14	1	1	1	1	2
Elected city	2	1	2	2	3	2	2	2	3	2	4	3	3
Business	3	6	6	5	2	3	5.5	4	2	5	3	6	4
Appointed county	4	4	9	8	7	5	8	5	7	6	7	10.5	5
Ad hoc	9	8	3	4	10	13.5	5.5	6	6	9	6	4	6
Non-affiliated	6	3	4.5	3	9	4	12.5	12	20	9	16.5	10.5	7
State	8	5	7	7	5	7	10	7.5	9	7	11	7.5	8
Professional	7	9	8	11.5	4	8	4	7.5	11	11	14.5	9	9
Civic	14	7	4.5	10	14.5	9	11	13	13	9	9	12	10
Federal	13	21.5	18	11.5	8	6	3	3	11	13.5	16.5	15	11
Communications	22	20	21	21	16.5	17	21.5	20.5	4.5	4	5	2	12.5
School	10	18.5	11	9	11	11.5	14	11	11	19	20.5	13	12.5
Local intergovernmental	16.5	11	13	14.5	18	19	12.5	9	20	19	20.5	24	14
Court	12	13	14	14.5	16.5	15.5	9	10	23.5	19	20.5	24	15
Civil rights	11	24	15.5	13	12	11.5	15.5	15.5	8	19	8	15	16

[a]This column rank orders actors for *all* interactions, irrespective of mode or quartile, in the 32 cases.

have, of course, been anticipated in the previous chapter, though without analysis by mode, and need not be repeated here.[2] Note, however, that unspecified individuals, absent as a category in Chapter III, can now be seen, not unexpectedly, to be linked predominantly with public statements. As individuals who approximate a general public, they naturally assume the fairly passive role of receivers of messages sent by more specialized actors. But this is not their sole activity. Some of them, for example, send messages to particular target audiences. Some also attend meetings of various government and non-government organizations. The appearance of unspecified individuals at meetings, while less common than their reception of public statements, occurs more frequently than similar appearances by civil rights representatives, spokesmen for religious bodies, or members of organized labor.[3]

Other actors in Table IV.1 also show prominent mode specialization. As might be expected, the communications industry concentrates on public statements, particularly through editorials and the interpretive reporting of news. Professional personnel rank much higher as senders and receivers of messages than as issuers of public statements. These differences can be traced to the different functional relationships of the actors to the decision process. The stock and trade of the press, after all, is the dissemination of views and information.[4] The participation of professional personnel, to the contrary, often involves letters and other communications from the government agency that hired them to conduct technical research, and reports to that body. Professional personnel also rank relatively high in attendance at meetings, since they assemble to discuss information and since they also are likely to appear at government sessions. Obviously, as Table IV.1 shows, professionals do issue some

[2] See Table III.5. Obviously, there are some differences. For example, appointed county ranks 5 here and 9 there; school, 12.5 and 6.5; professional, 9 and 5. These differences reflect the distinct bases of analysis in the two chapters—the mean of case percentages in Chapter III as against the aggregate of individual interactions in the present chapter. But the disparities should not be exaggerated. Indeed, the rank order correlation coefficient for the 23 actors listed in Table III.5 and the corresponding categories by the present method is a very high Spearman's rho of +.959. (Unspecified and non-affiliated actors are dropped from this computation, since they are not listed in Table III.5. Seven other actors, omitted from Table IV.1, *are* used in the computation.) Clearly, the two methods of counting are tapping the same kinds of phenomena.

[3] Furthermore, we have undoubtedly underestimated the presence of unspecified or public actors at meetings of various councils and boards. Even when such sessions are not closed, we do not record their presence unless the case authors specially tell us about it.

[4] The press is coded as an actor in public statements only if it appears to have originated their substance. Straight news reporting—for example, the text of a speech, the summary of an announcement, a chronicle of events—or a letter to the editor is credited in coding to the initiator of the content.

public statements, too; typically, however, it is their government sponsor that communicates to the general public.

In addition, for what in part are methodological reasons, federal officials are far more prominent as senders and receivers of messages than as participants at meetings or makers of public announcements. Undoubtedly, federal officials do attend meetings that affect local outcomes, but these are frequently not detected by a case writer focusing upon the metropolitan setting. Similarly, though they regularly issue public statements, most are not relevant to the case being described.[5]

Despite these and some lesser exceptions, for most actors the frequency with which they employ one mode of communication is a fairly good indicator of the extent to which they use the other two modes. This holds true both for such government actors as state and elected city officials and for representatives of such non-government interests as business and civic associations. Within every quartile each of these participant classifications tends to communicate through messages at about the same relative level as it does through meetings or public statements.

TABLE IV.2

Participation Rates of Actor Combinations Vary More by Mode than by Time

	Percentage of Interactions in Quartile				*in All*
	1	*2*	*3*	*4*	*Quartiles*
Meetings					
Government only	53	50	43	48	48
Organized non-government only	20	20	22	18	19
Both	22	24	32	28	27
Messages					
Government only	44	50	49	47	48
Organized non-government only	14	12	10	13	12
Both	41	34	41	39	39
Public statements					
Government only	43	57	46	42	46
Organized non-government only	53	37	42	51	47
Both	3	5	11	5	6

Percentages refer to the proportion of interactions within each mode quartile across the 32-case sample that exhibits the designated actor combination. Column totals can depart noticeably from 100 per cent because some interactions, e.g., among neighbors, involve neither government personnel nor *organized* non-government interests.

[5] The occasional interventions of federal personnel in metropolitan decision-making, instead, may seem to local participants, particularly local officials, unnecessarily capricious and troublesome. See especially Scott Greer, *Urban Renewal and American Cities* (Indianapolis: Bobbs-Merrill, 1965), ch. 5.

In Table IV.2, the more detailed actor categories have been classified as either government or non-government. The first heading includes elected and appointed officials at the city, county, and suburban levels, state and federal officials, members of intergovernmental boards at the local or state-local level, judicial personnel, members of governmentally appointed planning and sounding boards, and other government officials. The second heading embraces the categories of business, labor, professions, communications, civic, religion, civil rights, and party organization, as well as *ad hoc* groups. The two classifications of actors yield three configurations: government only, organized non-government only, and both.[6]

Combining actors into three types proceeds, of course, on the assumption that these have differing rates of interaction and are associated in identifiably characteristic ways with various aspects of the communicative process. As Table IV.2 shows, nearly half of all interactions, irrespective of mode, contain government personnel exclusively. Representatives of non-government, though, are no less active than those of government in issuing public statements. Indeed, in quartiles one and four they initiate communications to broad publics more frequently than do government actors. Meetings and messages of organized non-government alone, however, occur at a noticeably lower rate, while those that involve both kinds of actors occupy a middle position in each quartile.[7]

The stability of the distributions over time is striking. Admittedly, meetings between government and non-government personnel are proportionally lowest during the first two quartiles of cases, and messages exchanged between the two groups also fall off in the second period. Otherwise, the access of unofficial interests to government does not appear to be strongly influenced by time. Indeed, the sole remaining temporal deviation of note in Table IV.2 is a relative decline in the incidence of public statements by non-government actors in the second quartile, accompanied by a corresponding rise in such statements by government spokesmen.

Tables IV.3 through IV.6 show, by quartile and mode, the degree to which special circumstances like non-local settings, permeability extremes, informality, and levels of continuity are associated with the interaction behavior of government and non-government actors. These tables undertake comparison by subtraction from the "uncontrolled" percentages in Table IV.2. For each mode quartile cell, the direction of the differ-

[6] A few interactions, less than 3 per cent of the total, are excluded since they contain neither government nor organized non-government actors, but only unspecified or non-affiliated individuals. In addition, the appearance of such persons at other interactions is not recorded here and does not affect the classifications employed.

[7] In practice, very few public statements are ever jointly issued by representatives of both government and organized non-government.

TABLE IV.3

Non-Local Interactions Consistently Tend To Be Governmental

	Percentage Differences in Quartile				*in All Quartiles*
	1	*2*	*3*	*4*	
Non-local meetings					
Government only	+17	+14	+24	+16	+17
Organized non-government only	− 5	−16	−12	−13	−13
Both	− 7	+ 8	− 8	+ 1	− 1
Non-local messages					
Government only	− 5	+14	+23	+18	+16
Organized non-government only	+ 1	− 7	−10	− 7	− 7
Both	+ 4	− 4	−13	−10	− 8
Non-local public statements					
Government only	+44	+12	+38	+31	+29
Organized non-government only	−40	−19	−26	−25	−26
Both	− 3	+15	−11	− 1	− 1

Figures in this table represent differences between participation rates of actor combinations in all meetings, messages, and public statements and in non-local ones. Plus signs indicate higher percentages than those recorded for all meetings, messages, and public statements, and minus signs lower percentages (see Table IV.2). The numbers denote the extent of the departure. Columns do not total zero for the reason given in the note to Table IV.2.

ence is indicated by a plus or minus sign, while the number represents the magnitude of the deviation.[8]

As Table IV.3 indicates, all three modes of non-local interaction—meetings, messages, and public statements—show greater than usual rates for communications involving only government personnel and lower frequencies for those with persons exclusively from organized non-government. Outside the metropolitan area, government officials particularly dominate the issuance of public statements. The rows in Table IV.3 tend with considerable consistency to either exceed or to fall short of the mode quartile norms: only six of the forty-five figures are "out of order" with respect to sign. Quartile two shows the greatest difference in this respect, with access meetings (those containing both government and non-government actors) and jointly issued public statements occurring far more often than is customary. Access interactions, in other words, tend to take place somewhat earlier outside the city than is true in general.

Close inspection of the raw data would show that four cases—Mowitz-Airport, Crain-New Orleans, Mowitz-Gratiot, and Peabody-Tax—contribute by far the greatest number of non-local interactions in

[8] Similarly, Tables IV.8 and IV.9 are compared with Table IV.7; IV.11, with IV.10; and IV.13 through IV.15, with IV.12.

our sample. Their variety in subject matter is worth noting. They concern, respectively, the construction of a metropolitan airport that required state and federal cooperation, interference by the government at Baton Rouge in the desegregation problems of New Orleans, federal aid for an early urban renewal case in Detroit, and efforts by the city of Seattle to obtain new tax authorization from the state government. In three of the four cases the cities were seeking something of value for themselves, though the objects of their search varied considerably. Only in New Orleans was the city under severe pressure from the outside.

TABLE IV.4

Both Closed and Wide Open Meetings Exhibit Distinctive Participation Rates for Actor Combinations

	Percentage Differences in Quartile				*in All*
	1	*2*	*3*	*4*	*Quartiles*
Impermeable meetings					
Government only	− 2	−16	−17	− 7	−10
Organized non-government only	− 2	+ 4	+ 8	+ 4	+ 4
Both	+ 7	+ 7	+13	+ 8	+ 9
Fully permeable meetings					
Government only	−45	−37	−31	−31	−35
Organized non-government only	+ 6	0	+ 1	+ 4	+ 3
Both	+20	+28	+14	+10	+15

Figures in this table represent differences between participation rates of actor combinations in all meetings and in impermeable and permeable ones. Plus signs indicate higher percentages than those recorded for all meetings, and minus signs lower percentages (see Table IV.2). The numbers denote the extent of the departure. Columns do not total zero for the reason given in the note to Table IV.2.

As Table IV.4 shows, the percentage of exclusively governmental meetings is markedly reduced under conditions of both impermeability and full permeability. By contrast, meetings that are either completely open or completely closed show particularly frequent appearances of actors from both government and organized non-government. Very likely, the tendency for access meetings to occur in private reflects the fact that under such circumstances candid opinions and real demands can more often be expeditiously expressed.[9]

Fully permeable meetings that include government officials alone are quite rare. Generally, they occur only in order to ward off threats to local

[9] The present discussion, of course, concerns relative differences, not absolute rates. For example, a comparison of Tables IV.2 and IV.4 would show that the depression in the incidence of impermeable meetings of government alone does not mean such sessions were uncommon. Indeed, over the 32 case samples they were nearly as frequent as impermeable access meetings.

values, such as those posed by the location of a new airport. The increase in the attendance rates for open meetings by both actor groupings together, moreover, should be interpreted with some caution. For government officials often attend public gatherings only in token force, and sometimes government is represented solely by members of the police.

TABLE IV.5

Informal Meetings and Messages Exhibit Distinctive Participation Rates for Actor Combinations

	Percentage Differences in Quartile				*in All Quartiles*
	1	*2*	*3*	*4*	
Informal meetings					
Government only	−18	−18	−15	−14	−18
Organized non-government only	+11	+ 4	+ 7	+ 6	+ 7
Both	+11	+ 6	+21	+ 8	+11
Informal messages					
Government only	− 9	−26	−16	−19	−18
Organized non-government only	+18	+14	+16	+23	+19
Both	−13	− 8	0	− 5	− 7

Figures in this table represent differences between participation rates of actor combinations in all meetings and messages and in informal ones. Plus signs indicate higher percentages than those recorded for all meetings and messages, and minus signs lower percentages (see Table IV.2). The numbers denote the extent of the departure. Columns do not total zero for the reason given in the note to Table IV.2.

A diminished role for government officials is also evident when informal meetings are examined separately. As Table IV.5 indicates, during every quartile a far smaller than usual proportion of meetings that are spontaneous and off-the-record have exclusively government participation. It is characteristically democratic, after all, for many government activities to be carried on at least partially in a planned and recorded manner.[10] Business and other organized non-government interests are apparently more accustomed to informal sessions. Meetings that join government and outside interests, however, show the highest rates of increase. The jump of 21 per cent in quartile three is particularly striking and probably does not represent a spurious finding. Indeed, both logic and empirical evidence suggest that hard bargaining between government and other interests quite often takes place in an informal manner.[11]

[10] Much informal decision-making, either within government or between it and outside interests, constitutes what S. E. Finer has termed an "anonymous empire," not because it is secret but because nobody pays it much attention. In its routine detail it is often quite dull.

[11] A closer examination of this process is made in Table IV.19.

The trend lines for informal messages are also quite uniform. Government personnel constitute both sender and receiver of such messages less frequently than is customary, while organized non-government shows a comparable increase in rates. The fact that informal messages between the government and outside interests drop below the usual rates, while meetings between both groupings consistently exceed them, merely indicates how much greater the difficulty is in circulating informal communiques between organizations than in holding informal sessions attended by their various representatives. It is also ordinarily far safer to talk than to reduce positions to paper.

Table IV.6, in what is unfortunately a somewhat lengthy array, provides evidence about the distinctiveness of actor combinations by mode

TABLE IV.6

Participation Rates for Actor Combinations Vary More Directly with Continuity than with Time or Mode

	Percentage Differences in Quartile				*in All*
	1	*2*	*3*	*4*	*Quartiles*
			Regular Interactions		
Meetings					
Government only	+26	+18	+30	+25	+24
Organized non-government only	−12	− 4	−10	− 6	− 8
Both	−14	−16	−24	−18	−19
Messages					
Government only	+21	+21	+30	+36	+27
Organized non-government only	− 2	− 3	+ 1	− 5	− 3
Both	−18	−22	−30	−30	−26
Public statements					
Government only	+19	+18	+15	+14	+16
Organized non-government only	−17	−15	−10	− 9	−12
Both	− 1	− 2	− 3	− 2	− 2
			Case-Patterned Interactions		
Meetings					
Government only	− 6	+ 1	−15	−15	−12
Organized non-government only	+ 8	+ 7	+ 2	+ 2	+ 4
Both	+ 3	− 2	+17	+16	+12
Messages					
Government only	−20	−13	− 7	− 9	−10
Organized non-government only	− 3	− 2	0	− 4	− 2
Both	+23	+19	+ 7	+13	+14
Public statements					
Government only	−43	−50	−16	−35	−35
Organized non-government only	+40	+48	+28	+24	+33
Both	+ 4	− 5	−11	+ 6	0

TABLE IV.6–Continued

	Percentage Differences in Quartile 1	2	3	4	in All Quartiles
	Ephemeral Interactions				
Meetings					
Government only	−35	−33	−30	−23	−29
Organized non-government only	+17	+ 3	+13	+ 7	+ 9
Both	+21	+31	+19	+17	+20
Messages					
Government only	−14	−16	−21	−22	−19
Organized non-government only	+ 6	+ 7	− 1	+10	+ 6
Both	+ 6	+12	+22	+12	+14
Public statements					
Government only	−31	−52	−37	−35	−38
Organized non-government only	+28	+39	+19	+23	+25
Both	0	+10	+15	+ 4	+ 8

Figures in this table represent differences between participation rates of actor combinations in all meetings, messages, and public statements and in regular, case patterned, and ephemeral ones. Plus signs indicate higher percentages than those recorded for all meetings, messages, and public statements, and minus signs lower percentages (see Table IV.2). The numbers denote the extent of the departure. Columns do not total zero for the reason given in the note to Table IV.2.

and by all three levels of continuity. Throughout the four time periods, government is by far the most conspicuous participant in regular interactions, no matter what the mode. Organized non-government consistently tends to be just a bit underrepresented in regular meetings and messages, while combinations of government and outside interests are always markedly depressed.[12]

Case patterned and ephemeral interactions that include only government occur at lower than normal rates. Indeed, with but one exception, all figures for government alone in these two continuity categories have a negative sign in every quartile. Again, with only a single exception, case patterned and unpatterned meetings and messages tend to contain representatives of *both* government and organized non-government at higher rates than usual.[13] Indeed, throughout the four quartiles, approximately half the ephemeral (i.e., idiosyncratic) meetings involve access between the government and interests outside it. For the decision processes memorialized by our case sample, in other words, stable patterns of interaction between organized private interests and government agencies are

[12] The last generalization does not hold for public statements; but as reference to Table IV.2 would indicate, few of them are ever issued jointly by the two groupings anyway.
[13] Jointly issued public statements, once again, comprise so small a percentage of the totals that slight inconsistencies need not be stressed.

relatively uncommon. Moreover, access networks that are recounted tend to be initiated during the issue controversy itself rather than before it.

CORRELATES OF PERMEABILITY

In this section and in the next two, aspects of interaction other than participant classifications provide the primary foci. Our aim is to examine attributes like permeability, formality, and continuity and to assess their interplay, in order to draw a more detailed picture, by mode and quartile, of the decision processes in our cases.

TABLE IV.7

Permeability Levels of Meetings and Messages Are Similar, But Both Show Some Temporal Trends

	Percentage of Interactions in Quartile				*in All*
	1	*2*	*3*	*4*	*Quartiles*
Meetings					
Impermeable	22	30	28	32	28
Partly permeable	62	57	55	49	55
Fully permeable	16	13	17	19	17
Messages					
Impermeable	26	24	21	29	25
Partly permeable	62	68	65	60	63
Fully permeable	12	8	14	11	12

Percentages refer to the proportion of interactions within each meeting quartile and message quartile across the 32-case sample that exhibits the designated degree of permeability. Columns total 100 per cent. Public statements are omitted from this table and from Tables IV.8 and IV.9. By definition, all such statements are fully permeable.

Table IV.7 presents overall frequencies of permeability levels for meetings and messages. In consonance with the gross data of Chapter III,[14] meetings that are partly permeable, i.e., that, while not characterized by a large or vocal audience, are not secret either, reveal themselves to predominate throughout the four quartiles. Over time, however, they do tend to drop from more than 60 per cent of the mode quartile total to less than 50 per cent.

Though other patterns in this table are more erratic, one can observe a slight increase over time in the rates of both impermeable and fully permeable meetings. Such trends are plausible. As cases proceed, partly permeable meetings, the kind that councils and boards as well as many organized interests typically hold, tend to diminish in importance. At the

[14] See Table III.9.

same time, a polarization in the visibility of meetings occurs.[15] Indeed, toward the end of narratives there is frequently an increase in the proportion of confidential planning and strategy sessions on one hand and of massive demonstrations on the other.[16]

An examination of the interaction data, case by case, reveals that impermeable communications—closed meetings and messages—occur with greatest frequency in Mowitz-Airport, where many government contacts both within and between agencies took place behind the scenes; in Muir-Houses, where a plan to erect metal dwellings in New Haven instigated many private meetings among residents of the threatened neighborhood, and also required a number of party caucuses by members of the Board of Aldermen in order to fashion an acceptable solution; in Crain-New Orleans, where chaotic mass demonstrations induced private and frightened meetings of school officials and minor economic notables after the fact; and in Davies-Village, where a threat to bring urban renewal to the western portion of Greenwich Village was met by rapid and secret maneuvering of the aroused residents. Fully permeable interactions—completely open meetings and messages—are especially prominent in Crain-New Orleans, Mowitz-Airport, Mowitz-Port, and Davies-West Side, though the sorts of interactions they comprise differ considerably from case to case. School desegregation in New Orleans occasioned many rowdy and cursing street demonstrations by that city's white population. The Detroit airport case and the urban renewal plans for Manhattan's West Side involved a large number of public hearings and other institutionalized mass meetings. The Port decision, however, scores high in this category only because it contains a large number of publicized messages by various city, county, and business officials. Obviously, the notion "fully permeable" is decidedly more heterogeneous than is "impermeable."

The relation of informality to impermeability levels is very similar for both meetings and messages. Closed interactions are strikingly more prevalent in every mode quartile under the conditions of informality in Table IV.8. As a comparison with Table IV.7 would show, about four of every five meetings, and more than nine of every ten messages, are private if they are informal. Correspondingly, informality rates among partly permeable meetings and messages fall away sharply. The much smaller depression among fully permeable meetings indicates a persistent undercurrent of open and informal encounters—in other words, of demonstra-

[15] Since three levels of permeability are coded, these generalizations are not statistically redundant. It would have been possible, for example, for impermeable meetings to increase but fully permeable ones markedly to decrease.

[16] The figures in Table III.9 somewhat masked these trends, since the data there did not sort out meetings from the other two communication modes. Messages, as Table IV.7 indicates, remain quite stable over time in their permeability, and public statements are always fully permeable.

TABLE IV.8

Most Informal Meetings and Messages Are Impermeable

	Percentage Differences in Quartile 1	*2*	*3*	*4*	*in All Quartiles*
Informal meetings					
Impermeable	+55	+57	+60	+47	+54
Partly permeable	−53	−49	−51	−45	−49
Fully permeable	− 2	− 8	− 9	−2	− 5
Informal messages					
Impermeable	+63	+71	+68	+64	+67
Partly permeable	−54	−63	−57	−53	−57
Fully permeable	− 9	− 8	−11	−11	−10

Figures in this table represent differences between percentage distributions on permeability for all meetings and messages and for informal ones. Plus signs indicate higher percentages than those recorded for all meetings and messages, and minus signs lower percentages (see Table IV.7). The numbers denote the extent of the departure. Columns total zero.

tions. If one again compares the data in Table IV.7 and IV.8, it is clear that these wide-open and wide-swinging sessions are most common in the first and the last quartiles.

A closer examination of meetings (Table IV.9) indicates that those following preestablished networks have a particular tendency to be partly

TABLE IV.9

The Permeability of Meetings Varies with Continuity

	Percentage Differences in Quartile 1	*2*	*3*	*4*	*in All Quartiles*
Regular meetings					
Impermeable	− 5	+ 4	− 6	+ 1	− 1
Partly permeable	+12	+ 7	+15	+12	+12
Fully permeable	−7	−11	− 9	−13	−11
Case-patterned meetings					
Impermeable	− 9	− 5	+ 6	+ 6	+ 3
Partly permeable	+25	+11	+ 5	+ 5	+ 8
Fully permeable	−16	− 6	−11	−11	−11
Ephemeral meetings					
Impermeable	+12	− 4	+ 3	− 7	0
Partly permeable	−31	−18	−26	−21	−24
Fully permeable	+19	+22	+23	+28	+24

Figures in this table represent differences between percentage distributions on permeability for all meetings and for regular, case patterned, and ephemeral ones. Plus signs indicate higher percentages than those recorded for all meetings, and minus signs lower percentages (see Table IV.7). The numbers denote the extent of the departure. Columns total zero.

permeable. This is easily understood. Government sessions, for example, though rarely dominated by the public, are ordinarily open to it. Case-patterned meetings show a similar tendency. Indeed, the distributions of differences for regular and case-patterned meetings are remarkably similar. Ephemeral meetings, however, exhibit very different characteristics. Within every quartile there is a marked decline in their rate of part permeability and a large rise in the incidence of full permeability. Moreover, a comparison with Table IV.7 would reveal that only about three in every ten idiosyncratic meetings are partly permeable, while the proportion of such sessions that are fully permeable—public hearings, demonstrations, mass conclaves, and the like—jumps to over 50 per cent.

These latter types of meetings are often colorful and exciting and easily lend themselves to vivid reporting. Even their statistics can seem impressive. For example, in Pomper-Fluoridation we learn:

> The Board of Estimate hearing was the highlight of the New York fluoridation controversy. City officials heard testimony over a 15½ hour period, lasting until 2:00 A.M. Two hundred and eighty-six witnesses were present, of whom 86, the majority in opposition, were eventually heard.[17]

Street demonstrations in their way are often no less impressive.

> The next day the teenagers did something about it. A mob variously estimated between one and three thousand swept through the New Orleans Civic Center and the state supreme court building, surged into City Hall, and then marched on the federal courts and the board of education building. Some New Orleans residents have tried to play down the events of this day and were irritated when we used the word "crisis," but school board members and school staff admitted to being genuinely frightened at the sight of the mob steaming down Carondelet Street toward them.[18]

Yet, however easy these monumental confrontations may be to remember, they clearly provide only a very small portion of the interactions in case narratives.

CORRELATES OF FORMALITY

As has already been foreshadowed in Chapter III,[19] informal interactions are rare within every mode quartile. Not only are all public statements by definition characterized by formality, this attribute is also

[17] Pomper-Fluoridation, p. 55. (Gerald Pomper, "The New York Fluoridation Dispute," in *Cases in State and Local Government,* Richard T. Frost, ed., © 1961, Prentice-Hall, Inc. By permission.)
[18] Crain-New Orleans, p. 66 (or see Robert L. Crain, *The Politics of School Desegregation* [Chicago: Aldine, 1968], p. 276).
[19] See Table III.10.

TABLE IV.10

Messages Are Even More Frequently Formal than Meetings

	Percentage of Interactions in Quartile				*in All*
	1	*2*	*3*	*4*	*Quartiles*
Meetings					
Formal	76	69	72	66	70
Informal	24	31	28	34	30
Messages					
Formal	85	84	90	84	86
Informal	15	16	10	16	14

Percentages refer to the proportion of interactions within each meeting quartile and message quartile across the 32-case sample that exhibits the designated level of formality. Columns total 100 per cent. Public statements are omitted from this table and from Table IV.11. By definition, all such statements are formal.

extremely common among messages, as Table IV.10 makes clear. Of the three modes, meetings exhibit the tone and order of formality with least frequency, but even here less than a third of the encounters in any given quartile are informal. Although Table IV.10 also suggests a slight decrease in the rate of formal meetings over time, the evenness of the temporal distributions remains most striking.

Clearly, as Table IV.11 demonstrates, impermeable meetings and impermeable messages are typically less formal than such communications in general. Away from the curious eye of the public, flexible and unrecorded bargaining normally takes place. While seven of every ten

TABLE IV.11

Formality Depresses the Incidence of Impermeable Meetings

	Percentage Differences in Quartile				*in All*
	1	*2*	*3*	*4*	*Quartiles*
Formal and impermeable					
Meetings	−48	−58	−59	−51	−54
Messages	−37	−47	−32	−37	−38
Formal and fully permeable					
Meetings	+ 4	+18	+16	+ 4	+ 8
Messages			*		

Figures in this table represent differences between percentage distributions on formality for all meetings and messages and for impermeable and fully permeable ones. Plus signs indicate higher percentages than those recorded for all meetings and messages, and minus signs lower percentages (see Table IV.10). The numbers denote the extent of the departure. Data are supplied for formal interactions only. Those for informal interactions are equal in magnitude and opposite in sign.

* Fully permeable messages closely resemble public statements and are almost always deemed formal.

meetings in our sample on average are formal, the same holds true for only one impermeable meeting in six. The tendency toward informality among private messages is similar but less overwhelming. Indeed, as a comparison with Table IV.10 indicates, nearly half of such messages are still deemed formal. This difference between meetings and messages should occasion no surprise. For when information is put into writing or communicated outside an immediate setting, it often becomes highly structured and inherently less capable of supple modification and change.[20]

In contrast to closed meetings, completely open ones exhibit a higher incidence of formality than do meetings as a whole. These latter differences, though, are relatively modest and vary noticeably from quartile to quartile. The reason for this is that the category "fully permeable meetings" contains a large proportion of two quite different sorts of encounters. On the one hand, it includes public hearings and auditorium-sized gatherings of organizations—sessions that are sufficiently prestructured and self-recording to be considered formal. On the other hand, this category encompasses mass demonstrations in streets and parks—events that are usually so amorphous and unfocused as to be deemed informal. Since these demonstrations tend to occur either quite early or quite late in a case rather than during the middle two quartiles,[21] differences from formality norms for impermeable meetings largely disappear in quartiles one and four.

Because of the close association between impermeable and informal communications, the same cases that provide the bulk of illustrations for the one characteristic also furnish most of those for the other. In addition, certain briefer cases possess relatively large numbers of informal meetings and messages. In Logue-Demotion, for example, a Deputy Chief Inspector of the New York Police Department, who had enforced certain anti-gambling ordinances too stringently, received many informal words of advice and reprimand from his superiors in the Department; in Keeley-Moses, fully a third of the interactions involved behind-the-scenes maneuvering and reconnoitering by residents who sought to prevent an automobile parking lot from being constructed in nearby Central Park; and in Banfield-Hall, many of the key decisions that led to the construction of McCormick Place occurred at bargaining sessions among leading businessmen of Chicago's Loop.

[20] Telephone calls provide the most obvious exception to this generalization (though even they can be monitored) and are consistently coded as informal. Written messages directed beyond a given organization and carrying its imprimatur are almost always adjudged formal. The coding of "unofficial" written communiques varies more or less with the probability of their finding their way into regular dossiers.

[21] See the discussion of Table IV.8.

CORRELATES OF CONTINUITY

The data in Table IV.12 help us begin a further inquiry into the relationship among various aspects of meetings, messages, and public statements. The frequencies of continuity levels presented in that table

TABLE IV.12

Continuity Varies More by Mode than by Time

	Percentage of Interactions in Quartile				*in All Quartiles*
	1	*2*	*3*	*4*	
Meetings					
Regular	53	53	43	44	47
Case patterned	15	17	27	25	22
Ephemeral	32	30	30	31	31
Messages					
Regular	43	41	30	29	35
Case patterned	27	32	41	39	35
Ephemeral	30	27	29	32	30
Public statements					
Regular	65	74	67	71	70
Case patterned	12	10	11	11	11
Ephemeral	23	16	22	18	19

Percentages refer to the proportion of interactions within each mode quartile across the 32-case sample that exhibits the designated level of continuity. Columns total 100 per cent.

evince both notable disparities from one mode of interaction to another and noteworthy stabilities across the quartiles of any given mode. The employment of regular (or preestablished) communication channels, for example, is far more usual for public statements than for meetings; the gap in interaction regularity is even greater between public statements and messages. By contrast, the proportion of public statements that are case patterned is only about half that for meetings and less than a third that for messages.

Temporal uniformity within each interaction mode warrants perhaps more attention. For example, about seven of every ten public statements in our 32-case sample are issued by persons such as government officials, spokesmen for the Chamber of Commerce, and editorial writers, who persistently make such announcements. In no quartile does this proportion fall below 65 per cent or rise above 75 per cent. Rates for newly patterned and unpatterned public statements also remain quite stable.

Admittedly, for meetings and messages certain temporal trends can be discerned. In particular, these interactions keep somewhat less to regular channels as decision processes pass their midpoint, and instead tend more to follow paths that have been constructed during the case itself. Such differences, however, are fairly small. Furthermore, those unusual or idiosyncratic meetings and messages we have labeled ephemeral occur at nearly uniform rates in all four quartiles.

One might well have expected a far sharper rise over time in the incidence of case-patterned communications and a much steeper plunge in ephemeral ones. In this way issue controversies would be carried along during their first half by ordinary means and by occasional and sporadic interventions. Only in the latter stages of a decision would newly permanent interaction patterns take hold. To a slight extent, as the previous paragraph mentions, the data do uphold these predictions. Initial rates for case-patterned communications, however, are not unusually low, nor do the proportions in the fourth quartile loom much larger than those for all quartiles combined. Case patterning obviously can occur quite early, and, as the previous chapter also indicates,[22] apparently can reach its peak before the final period.

The consistency with which approximately three of ten meetings or messages are unprecedented in their actor configurations should occasion even more surprise. Indeed, were the excellent scripts of cases fictional, they might readily be criticized as poor dramatic vehicles. Too many new participants or combinations of participants find their way onto the stage during the fourth act. The text of a "well-made play" would have exhibited a marked decline in the rate of these ephemeral interactions as the drama unfolds. As Table IV.12 makes clear, though, newness in these narratives is constantly being replenished either as those who have not previously contacted one another exchange information or as those who have not previously been "in the know" realize something is happening.[23]

As one might reasonably expect, interactions illustrating regular networks that predate controversies tend to come in greatest numbers from the lengthiest cases. These include Mowitz-Airport, Crain-New Orleans, and Davies-Rockaway. In addition, Mowitz-Water, an account of the struggles between city and county officials over who should supply water outside the city of Detroit, also has an abundance of regular communications, even though it contains only 95 interactions. Except for Mowitz-Airport, the five narratives that contribute the most case-patterned interactions differ completely from the previous list. They include Mowitz-Gratiot, Mowitz-Corktown, Birkhead-Report, and Mowitz-

[22] See Table III.11.

[23] The slight decline in the rate of ephemeral interactions over time that Table III.11 reports is due in part to its different analytic basis, in part to its inclusion of public statements.

Expressway.[24] The five cases that bulk largest in ephemeral interactions include (in addition, once again, to Mowitz-Airport) Davies-Rockaway, Davies-Village, Banfield-Hall, and Muir-Houses. Three of the five involved threats to neighborhoods posed by possible new residential construction. Such intrusions seem likely to yield large numbers of sporadic and relatively unpatterned responses from residents.

TABLE IV.13

Continuity Varies Irregularly by Time and Mode in Non-Local Interactions

	Percentage Differences in Quartile				*in All*
	1	*2*	*3*	*4*	*Quartiles*
Non-local meetings					
Regular	+ 2	+ 8	− 5	+27	+12
Case patterned	− 5	−10	− 8	−12	− 9
Ephemeral	+ 3	+ 2	+13	−15	− 3
Non-local messages					
Regular	− 8	− 8	− 3	− 3	− 6
Case patterned	+13	+ 2	+19	+ 9	+12
Ephemeral	− 5	+ 6	−16	− 6	− 6
Non-local public statements					
Regular	+22	+ 7	+16	+19	+17
Case patterned	−12	+ 2	− 2	− 8	− 5
Ephemeral	−10	− 9	−14	−11	−12

Figures in this table represent differences between percentage distributions on continuity for all meetings, messages, and public statements and for non-local ones. Plus signs indicate higher percentages than those recorded for all meetings, messages, and public statements, and minus signs lower percentages (see Table IV.12). The numbers denote the extent of the departure. Columns total zero.

The relationship between non-local settings and continuity levels in the three modes is shown in Table IV.13. Meetings and public statements that have their locus outside the metropolitan area, and that are directly relevant to a metropolitan issue, tend to employ preestablished communications links at higher rates than usual. Such prior networks are especially pronounced for meetings in the final quartile, where a last-ditch effort by actors who have long been in communication with one another may often be made in order to save a project that appears jeopardized. Among non-local messages, however, case patterning shows a consistent increase.

[24] The four Detroit cases may perhaps be indicative of their authors' talents as well as of Detroit's politics. Their diversity of content—two concern urban renewal, one an airport, and the last a highway extension—precludes their high incidences of case-patterned interactions being explained in terms of any single issue.

Indeed, the jump of 19 per cent in quartile three changes their rate to fully six out of ten.[25] For those cases that require messages from outside the city, then, the third quartile often seems the time when persons who have not habitually been in mutual contact begin to establish persistent communication linkages.[26]

TABLE IV.14

Fully Permeable Meetings Exhibit Distinctive Continuity Levels

	Percentage Differences in Quartile				*in All*
	1	*2*	*3*	*4*	*Quartiles*
Impermeable meetings					
Regular	−17	+ 8	−10	+ 1	− 3
Case patterned	+ 7	− 3	+ 6	+ 6	+ 4
Ephemeral	+10	− 5	+ 4	− 7	− 1
Fully permeable meetings					
Regular	−24	−43	−23	−30	−30
Case patterned	−15	− 8	−17	−15	−14
Ephemeral	+39	+51	+40	+45	+44

Figures in this table represent differences between percentage distributions on continuity for all meetings and for impermeable and fully permeable ones. Plus signs indicate higher percentages than those recorded for all meetings, and minus signs lower percentages (see Table IV.12). The numbers denote the extent of the departure. Columns total zero.

Among meetings, impermeability and continuity levels stand in an interesting relationship, as the quartile distributions in Table IV.14 indicate. For example, the proportion of closed meetings that are regular is heightened in quartile two, though it is depressed in both the first and third quartiles. As an earlier investigation of Detroit indicated,[27] the second quartile is often the time action in cases turns inward. Government organizations then discuss problems internally or with other government

[25] Since messages frequently occur in pairs, with senders and receivers reversed, while meetings and public statements require no such symmetry, messages naturally tend to show a higher rate of case patterning than either of the other two modes. This fact has already been noted in our discussions of Table IV.12. What is important here is that the proportion of case patterned, non-local messages in quartile three is 19 per cent higher than the comparable, very high figure of 41 per cent.

[26] Very often these persons are officials at different levels of government. See Table IV.3.

[27] See Morris Davis, "Some Aspects of Detroit's Decisional Profile," *Administrative Science Quarterly,* 12 (1967), 209–24. The article employs a less comprehensive code than the one used in this book, and its data base rests only in the seven Detroit cases by Mowitz and Wright. Despite these substantive and methodological differences, it contains many findings that are congruent, both in general and in detail, with the conclusions reached here.

offices with which they are normally in contact. Private groups also engage in strategic or tactical planning during this period. Conversely, case-patterned impermeable meetings, which show small increases in every other quartile, dip slightly during the second. Indeed, a comparison with the data in Table IV.12 would show that newly patterned private meetings occur during the second quartile at less than half the rate attained during the remainder of the cases.

While the interquartile figures for fully permeable meetings in Table IV.14 are more obviously consistent, they are for that reason also less interesting. By their nature, open sessions are rarely case patterned and are regular in continuity even less often.[28] As a consequence, three of four meetings that are fully permeable are ephemeral. The findings are clear but expectable, in contrast to the weaker but more theoretically important differences for impermeable meetings.

TABLE IV.15

Informal Meetings Tend Not To Follow Old Networks, While Informal Messages Tend Not To Follow New Ones

	Percentage Differences in Quartile				*in All Quartiles*
	1	*2*	*3*	*4*	
Informal meetings					
Regular	−28	+ 1	−18	−11	−13
Case patterned	+10	− 4	+ 7	+ 4	+ 4
Ephemeral	+18	+ 3	+11	+ 7	+ 9
Informal messages					
Regular	− 8	+11	+ 7	+ 8	+ 6
Case patterned	+ 2	− 8	− 4	−22	−11
Ephemeral	+ 6	− 3	− 3	+14	+ 5

Figures in this table represent differences between percentage distributions on continuity for all meetings and messages and for informal ones. Plus signs indicate higher percentages than those recorded for all meetings and messages, and minus signs lower percentages (see Table IV.12). The numbers denote the extent of the departure. Columns total zero.

Finally, as Table IV.15 reveals, informal meetings are associated with continuity levels in an interesting manner. Though initially it may appear odd, informality increases the likelihood of actors' being brought together in unprecedented configurations. Except for the second quartile, where intra-organizational communication increases in frequency,[29] informal meetings involve regular, on-going networks at lower than usual

[28] A series of mass meetings rarely contains actor configurations similar enough among sessions to constitute a single pattern.
[29] See the discussion of Table IV.14 just above.

rates. The trend lines for messages clearly differ from those for meetings and also show considerable temporal irregularity. More than is usual, communiques that are informal utilize either regular channels that pre-date cases or idiosyncratic linkages that do not become stabilized. The increased rate in quartile four of informal messages that travel along previously untrod paths is especially worthy of notice. It reflects perhaps the crises that often erupt toward the end of narratives and that eventuate in sporadic interactions.

Analyses in this section and the preceding two have shown how strongly many aspects of interaction are related, especially within particular modes and quartiles. Given levels of each of the four characteristics focused upon—locale, permeability, formality, and continuity—are clearly more prevalent in the presence of specifiable levels of the others. Since these associations of attributes seem to reflect quite distinctive components in decision processes, they deserve some further attention. In addition, the actor categories with which we began this chapter can now be reintroduced in order that we may examine more closely the extent to which various participants appear not only in modes but in certain precisely defined interaction configurations.

COMMUNICATIONS AMONG ACTORS

Because of their obvious implications for policy formation, communications among different levels and agencies of government, and between government and outside interests, have long concerned political scientists. In this section we shall look first at the more traditional of these two concerns, intergovernmental relations, and then at the way in which selected non-government actors in our case sample demonstrate access-related participation.

Table IV.16 focuses upon intergovernmental meetings. Its most notable characteristic is a numerical paucity. Indeed, government meetings that cross levels account for only about 19 per cent of the exclusively government meetings in our sample. More than four of every five government sessions, in other words, have persons from only a single level of government present. Without doubt, the United States possesses an actively functioning federal system; but in the working out of metropolitan decisions, even major and controversial ones like those typically recorded in case studies, meetings in which planning and determining are accomplished apparently take place mainly within one level of government.[30]

[30] An even larger proportion of messages that involve "government only" circulate wholly within one government level.

TABLE IV.16

Meetings Involving Intergovernmental Pairs Typically Decrease with Distance from the Central City

	City	County	State	Local Intergovernmental	Federal	Court	School
City		37	33	21	9	11	3
County			19	14	7	1	4
State				2	8	4	7
Local Intergovernmental					3	0	0
Federal						3	1
Court							7
School							
Totals	114	82	73	40	31	26	22
All	388						

Meetings that contain actors from only one of the categories in this table are omitted as being *intra*governmental. Meetings that contain actors from two categories have one pairing, those with three categories have three pairings, those with four categories have six pairings.

The progression of totals in Table IV.16 follows the geographical distance of actors from the core city. Thus, participation in pairings declines as one reads down the bottom diagonal from city to county, state, local intergovernmental, and finally federal.[31] Two specialized government units, the courts and the schools, complete the list.[32] A similar tendency can be observed within the matrix cells for city or county personnel. Though the remaining figures are too small to warrant detailed analysis, one should perhaps note that the rather conspicuous numbers of meetings between school officials on the one hand and representatives of the state or of the courts on the other derive from the school desegregation controversy described in Crain-New Orleans.

Tables IV.17 through IV.19 analyze the more plentiful data in our case sample that concern the access-related activities of various private interests. The actor roles, arrayed in these tables in terms of total activity, encompass business, *ad hoc,* professional, civic, civil rights, religion and labor. The categories of participation are also listed so that the weakest or most diffuse endeavors—those that usually imply the least influence on government—are at the top of the table, while the most intimate communication activities are at the bottom.

The various kinds of participation can be briefly described. Anomic protests include impermeable, informal meetings such as riots. Public statements by definition are fully permeable, formal announcements. Open sessions with government refer to fully permeable, formal meetings attended by representatives of both government and non-government.[33] These embrace public hearings at which non-government actors appear as well as mass meetings of non-government groups at which any government representatives are present. Open messages to government include all partly or fully permeable messages sent by non-government to government actors. Open messages from government are similar to the foregoing, except the direction is reversed. Relatively open meetings with government refer to all sessions at which government and non-government actors are present and which are partly permeable. The presence of a civil rights representative at a city council meeting exemplifies the category. Closed messages to and from government are distinguished by

[31] A matrix for intergovernmental messages, not presented here, would show distance from the core city a far less consistent predictor of pairing rates. This is to be expected. After all, one salient feature of mediated communication is its overcoming of spatial separation. Indeed, messages between city and *federal* officials constitute the most frequent kind of intergovernmental activity at a distance.

[32] To increase the clarity of Table IV.16, data on suburban officials and persons in the residual category "other governmental" have been omitted. None of these actors appeared in many pairs.

[33] Non-government hereafter refers only to the seven actor categories specified in Tables IV.17 through IV.19.

TABLE IV.17

Most Non-Governmental Interests Emphasize Similar Access-Related Activities

Category of Participation	*Percentage of Interactions by Actor*						
	Business	*Ad hoc*	Professional	Civic	Civil Rights	Religion	Labor
Anomic protests	0	7	0	2	10	1	0
Public statements	28	30	18	33	33	36	44
Open sessions with government	7	16	12	19	12	7	15
Open messages to government	21	19	23	22	29	25	15
Open messages from government	12	6	17	4	6	7	8
Relatively open meetings with government	12	10	13	11	5	9	10
Closed messages to and from government	8	3	8	1	1	5	0
Formal, closed meetings with government	1	1	1	0	0	0	0
Unusual, closed, informal meetings with government	4	3	4	4	2	6	8
Case patterned or usual, closed, informal meetings with government	7	5	4	4	2	4	0
	N = 356	232	206	132	118	90	39

Columns total 100 per cent. Categories of participation are defined in the text (pp. 68 and 70).

their impermeability. Formal closed meetings with government encompass those few impermeable but formal sessions in which bargaining is totally absent. Unusual, closed, informal meetings with government are simultaneously impermeable, informal, and also ephemeral. Finally, case patterned or usual, closed, informal meetings with government are similar to the previous category, except they are not ephemeral.

Parallels in participant activity clearly characterize Table IV.17. For example, about a third of the access-related participation by each actor classification consists of public statements.[34] A further 20 to 30 per cent comprises open messages to government. Relatively open meetings with government constitute about another 10 per cent. Attendance at open sessions with government varies somewhat more, but keeps within the range of 7 to 19 per cent. The remaining categories of participation all occur with far smaller frequencies.

As the sample sizes at the base of Table IV.17 indicate, labor is clearly the least prominent of the seven actor roles examined in its gross rate of political communications. Except perhaps for civil rights organizations, it also appears to be the least influential in terms of its interaction profile. These two role categories apart, the general impression from Table IV.17 is one of overall constancy in the mix of activities from actor to actor. Business, as we have often noted before,[35] plays a numerically greater part in political activity than do other non-government roles. What is surprising, however, is that the profiles of most of the actor classifications look so much alike.

Admittedly, Table IV.17 may slightly mislead, suggesting perhaps that the various role classifications have similar impacts on governance. In Table IV.18, where the categories of participation are treated independently, one can more clearly assess the character of the activities undertaken by each non-government role. Here, the extent to which business dominates interactions implying close connections with government is sharply revealed. In general, business percentages for the more intimate activities in the bottom half of Table IV.18 are higher than those in the top half. Furthermore, only business and professionals[36] receive far more open messages from government than they send to it. Anomic protest is

[34] The classification "professional" provides the sole exception. As noted earlier (see Table IV.1), engineers and other specialists often stand in a contractual relationship to government and leave public announcements of findings to their sponsoring agencies.

[35] See, for example, the discussion of Table IV.1. This type of finding has been validated by many community studies, whether they employ reputation, stratification, or case study approaches.

[36] As mentioned before, professionals in our sample of cases are frequently in government hire.

TABLE IV.18

Intimate Access-Related Activities Are Ordinarily Engaged in by Few Non-Governmental Interests

Percentage of Interactions by Category of Participation	*Actor*							
	Business	*Ad hoc*	Professional	Civic	Civil rights	Religion	Labor	N =
Anomic protests	0	48	0	10	39	3	0	31
Public statements	30	21	11	13	11	9	5	340
Open sessions with government	18	27	18	18	11	4	4	139
Open messages to government	28	18	19	11	13	9	2	258
Open messages from government	38	12	31	5	6	5	3	109
Relatively open meetings with government	35	19	21	11	5	6	3	125
Closed messages to and from government	45	13	29	3	2	8	0	60
Formal, closed meetings with government	50	13	37	0	0	0	0	8
Unusual, closed, informal meetings with government	33	17	17	11	4	11	7	46
Case patterned or usual, closed, informal meetings with government	46	21	14	9	3	7	0	57

Rows total 100 per cent. Categories of participation are defined in the text (pp. 68 and 70).

the sole category in which business fails to participate at a high level, an exception that obviously indicates strength rather than weakness.

Ad hoc groups have behavior impacts quite different from those of business. They are responsible for nearly half the anomic protests in our cases; they also characteristically attend public sessions with government at a substantial rate. Other roles such as labor, religion, civil rights, and civic are far weaker in their interactions with government. Even in the aggregate, they account for only 13 per cent of the closed messages exchanged with government, in contrast with business' 45 per cent, and for only 19 per cent of the regular bargaining sessions with government, in contrast with business' 46 per cent.

A better reason for treating Table IV.17 with caution is that it fails to distinguish the time periods during which the various actors engage in their forms of political participation. Table IV.19 expands the analysis by identifying the quartiles in which these communications occur. Clearly, business and those categories that more closely resemble it—*ad hoc,* professional, and civic[37]—not only have frequent close relationships with government but also establish them earlier and keep them more continuously. This generalization is particularly true for business, the only actor that has patterned, closed, informal meetings with government in all four quartiles.

As one moves from the first to the second quartile in Table IV.19, much critical activity tends to go underground or at least remains within organizations.[38] Intimate meetings between organized interests and government are again sparce, with the dearth spreading to *ad hoc* groups. Businessmen, however, and to a lesser degree professional personnel, continue to attend many closed, informal meetings with government. Indeed, business even increases its rate of appearance at such bargaining sessions, the frequency rising from 6 per cent in quartile one to 12 per cent in quartile two.

The third quartile shows actor participation profiles that closely resemble the distributions in the first quartile. In particular, persons representing civil rights, religion, and labor remain virtually absent from closed meetings with, or closed messages to, government. Not until quartile four do these latter organizations begin to come into close government contact.[39] During this final period, 16 per cent of the political communication

[37] *Ad hoc* groups usually contain either prominent business leaders who have banded under a new name for some particular issue or neighborhood property owners and entrepreneurs; professional personnel are often linked to important engineering or architecture firms; and civic associations normally have a large business component.

[38] See the discussion of Table IV.15.

[39] Labor, the weakest interest in these cases, does not achieve such contact even in the fourth quartile. Note also that civil rights, which was recorded as having an early

TABLE IV.19

Access-Related Activities Vary over Time for Most Non-Governmental Interests

Category of Participation	*Percentage of Interactions by Actor in Quartiles* Business				*Ad Hoc*				Professional				Civic				Civil rights				Religion				Labor			
	1	*2*	*3*	*4*	*1*	*2*	*3*	*4*	*1*	*2*	*3*	*4*	*1*	*2*	*3*	*4*	*1*	*2*	*3*	*4*	*1*	*2*	*3*	*4*	*1*	*2*	*3*	*4*
Anomic protests	0	0	0	0	9	0	7	7	0	0	0	0	7	0	5	0	8	0	3	23	*	6	0	0	0	0	0	0
Public statements	35	29	34	20	32	32	27	31	15	28	5	25	50	31	32	31	34	11	45	30		31	26	47	40	18	78	45
Open sessions with government	5	7	8	8	20	24	13	15	8	10	14	13	7	26	17	19	31	6	3	13		0	11	7	20	18	11	11
Open messages to government	15	16	25	23	12	16	22	20	21	24	30	20	7	20	24	26	23	55	34	15		38	33	17	20	9	11	22
Open messages from government	14	19	7	8	9	8	6	4	23	10	21	12	22	6	0	0	4	17	6	3		19	7	2	20	9	0	0
Relatively open meetings with government	14	11	11	13	3	12	8	13	15	7	12	14	0	11	12	12	0	11	6	5		6	19	2	0	18	0	22
Closed messages to and from government	8	5	5	11	3	8	4	2	5	10	9	9	0	3	0	2	0	0	0	3		0	0	9	0	0	0	0
Formal, closed meetings with government	3	1	0	1	3	0	0	0	5	0	0	1	0	0	0	0	0	0	0	0		0	0	0	0	0	0	0
Unusual, closed, informal meetings with government	3	5	3	5	6	0	3	4	3	11	5	1	0	3	5	5	0	0	3	3		0	4	9	0	28	0	0
Case patterned or usual, closed, informal meetings with government	3	7	7	11	3	0	10	4	5	0	4	5	7	0	5	5	0	0	0	5		0	0	7	0	0	0	0
N =	77	74	85	120	34	25	71	102	39	29	57	81	14	35	41	42	26	18	35	39	4	16	27	43	10	11	9	9

Columns total 100 per cent. Categories of participation are defined in the text (pp.68 and 70).
* This column is omitted in quartile one for having too few interactions.

by religious actors occurs at closed, informal meetings with government. The corresponding rates for civil rights and civic interests are 8 per cent and 10 per cent. The figures resemble those registered by business (16 per cent) and exceed those for professional groups.[40]

Since quartile four contains more interactions than any of the other time periods, it tends to dominate totals that are computed across entire cases. This fact largely accounts for the parallel patterning in Table IV.17. The more detailed analysis by quartile indicates that while non-business actors in civic, civil rights, and religious fields are in some instances *generally* active even toward the beginning of cases, their close ties to government are usually delayed until much later. Non-business groupings, in other words, are inducted into presumably more meaningful aspects of political decision-making only after processes are well under way. Unlike business, which establishes close relationships with government early, these non-government actors are privy to the intimate settings for political bargaining only after the course of events has largely been set and most options effectively precluded.

Without quartile analysis one would likely overestimate the impact of non-business participation. Even reputational approaches might exaggerate its importance, since late entry by an actor into an issue controversy is usually marked by considerable visibility and publicity. Quartile analysis thus helps in clarifying the status of various interests and their effect upon the governments they seek to influence.

PROPOSITIONAL SUMMARY

The analyses in this chapter support the following generalizations about metropolitan cases.

1. The rank of a given actor classification is usually similar for all three communication modes, although considerable mode specialization exists for such participants as professionals, federal officials, and the press.
2. Organized non-government actors participate by themselves in far fewer meetings and messages than do government officials, but both classifications are about equally prominent in the issuance of public statements.
3. Non-local interactions, whatever their mode, tend to involve government officials exclusively.

---

temporal participation score in Table III.7, can now be seen nonetheless to achieve *close* relations with government quite late. The activity of civil rights representatives throughout the first three quartiles is almost completely limited to issuing public statements, attending open sessions with government, and sending open messages to it.

[40] The latter have already made their reports and begun to retire from the scene.

4. Outside the central city, messages between government and organized non-government tend to occur quite early.
5. Government and non-government actors appear together with particular frequency at meetings that are either wholly restricted from the public or completely visible.
6. The fact that a meeting is either impermeable (closed) or fully permeable (open) reduces the likelihood of its being exclusively governmental.
7. Informal meetings are apparently conducive to interactions among organized non-government actors and between such persons and government officials.
8. Government officials by themselves play an especially prominent part in regular interactions of all three modes.
9. Case patterned and ephemeral meetings or messages occur with diminished frequency among government officials and with increased frequency between such officials and representatives of private interests.
10. Meetings and messages are most often partly permeable and least often fully permeable.
11. The proportion of meetings and messages that are closed is strikingly high when interactions are informal, while the rate for partly permeable meetings and messages is correspondingly low.
12. Regular and case-patterned meetings show a greater incidence of partial permeability, while ephemeral meetings are more frequently fully permeable.
13. Most meetings and messages are formal in tone; yet the incidence of informality rises substantially when they are also impermeable.
14. Public statements follow regular channels of communication far more often than do the other two modes; messages show the highest incidence of case patterning.
15. For both meetings and messages, case-patterned interactions tend to occur with greater frequency during the latter two quartiles.
16. The proportions of meetings and of messages that are ephemeral remain consistently similar over all four quartiles.
17. Meetings and public statements that occur in non-local settings show frequent regularity; non-local messages are characterized by case patterning.
18. During the second quartile, impermeable meetings exhibit pronounced regularity.

19. Throughout the time span of cases, and especially in the first quartile, informality is strongly associated with the ephemeral character of meetings; for messages the relation is notable only for the final quartile.
20. Intragovernmental meetings occur mainly within single levels of government.
21. The frequency with which representatives of various levels of government encounter officials of central cities and counties at meetings is a function largely of geographical distance.
22. Though the various non-government roles differ markedly in their incidence of access-related activities, most of them exhibit similar participation profiles.
23. Business partakes in the most intimate access-related activities, while civic and civil rights groups are mainly confined to public and diffuse gestures.
24. Business tends to sustain its close contacts with government throughout all time periods, while civil rights and religious actors usually enter into private, informal meetings with government in the last quartile.

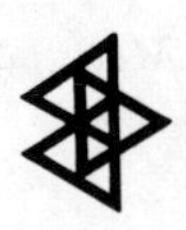

CHAPTER V

City and Issue Patterns

UNTIL NOW WE have refrained from analyzing our interaction data by either city or issue. To generalize from only a few sets of narratives obviously involves considerable risk. The hazards are compounded by the diversity of case authors, none of whom provides information about more than one topic for more than one locale. Nevertheless, many differences among places or issues remain open to illumination by our procedures. If, for example, New York City and Chicago manage decisions in sharply distinctive ways, or if airport location and school integration are handled through markedly divergent processes, even small numbers of cases should prove revealing. In any event, the promise of directly comparable data on cities and issues, at present so meager, encourages an effort similar to that in the two preceding chapters.[1]

INTERACTIONS IN CITIES

Table V.1 lists the six cities for which interaction data are sufficiently abundant to warrant close analysis. Each city's net total of case interactions is presented along with the abbreviated designation of the studies that contain them.[2] In addition to accounts from four metropolises—Chicago, Detroit, New York City, and Syracuse—the analysis also rests on nine narratives from Beloit, Wisconsin, and Oberlin, Ohio. Since these

[1] Because of the reduced number of interactions in the present chapter (see Tables V.1 and V.8), breakdowns by quartile will be made only in passing and will not be featured on any subsequent tables.

[2] As in Chapter IV, the analytic unit is the individual interaction, aggregated here by city or issue.

TABLE V.1

Interaction Totals and Case Sources for Six Cities

City	*Net Interaction Count*	*Abbreviated Designation of Cases*
Chicago	200	Banfield-Hall, Banfield-Project, Rossi-Hyde Park
Detroit	949	Mowitz-Airport, Mowitz-Building, Mowitz-Corktown, Mowitz-Expressway, Mowitz-Gratiot, Mowitz-Port, Mowitz-Water
New York	566	Davies-Rockaway, Davies-Village, Davies-West Side, Keeley-Moses, Logue-Demotion, Pomper-Fluoridation, Simon-Hospitals
Syracuse	226	Birkhead-Report, Herman-Sewage, Martin-Water
Beloit	139	Mills-Buses, Mills-Education, Mills-Fire, Mills-Zoning
Oberlin	274	Wildavsky-FAA, Wildavsky-Housing, Wildavsky-Negroes, Wildavsky-Water, Wildavsky-Zoning

For information about the case studies in Chicago, Detroit, New York City, and Syracuse, see Table III.1. The four Beloit cases are all in Warner E. Mills, Jr., and Harry R. Davis, *Small City Government* (New York: Random House, 1962), while the five Oberlin cases come from Aaron Wildavsky, *Leadership in a Small Town* (Totowa, N.J.: Bedminster Press, 1964). Titles, page references, net interaction counts, and time spans for these nine cases are as follows:

Abbreviated Designation	*Title and Page Reference*	*Net Interaction Count*	*Time Span (Yr.)*	*Time Span (Mo.)*
Mills-Buses	The Beloit Bus Crisis, 55–72	49		4
Mills-Education	The Van Horn Affair, 44–54	25		1
Mills-Fire	The Emergency Fire Protection Appropriation, 73–93	44		7
Mills-Zoning	The Case of the Crowded Corral, 16–30	21		9
Wildavsky-FAA	The Coming of the FAA, 143–49	32		1½
Wildavsky-Housing	The Housing Code, 83–99	42	1	
Wildavsky-Negroes	Negroes and Low-Cost Housing, 110–26	60	2	6
Wildavsky-Water	The Great Water Controversy, 52–71	76	1	1
Wildavsky-Zoning	Enforcement of the Zoning Ordinance, 127–42	64	2	7

two communities have populations of only about 33,000 and 8,000, respectively,[3] their inclusion should permit us to weigh, at least roughly, the influence of size on interaction aspects of urban decisions.

Obviously, the cases in Table V.1 are not randomly distributed across the locales. Detroit and New York City are represented by six and

[3] Although Oberlin is in fact a town rather than a city, we will refer to it as a city in order to avoid such infelicities as "five cities and a town."

seven narratives, respectively; Chicago and Syracuse have only three apiece. Furthermore, the 949 interactions in the Detroit material contrast with the 139 for Beloit. Variety and geographical scope of the issue controversies studied also differentiate the six cities. Cases in New York City, Detroit, Beloit, and Oberlin each depict a fairly broad range of topics, while accounts from Chicago or Syracuse tend to overlap considerably.[4] In addition, although several Detroit cases and two of the three from Syracuse deal with decisions that are essentially area-wide in character, the remaining narratives—including all those from Chicago, New York City, Beloit, and Oberlin—treat problems faced primarily by the central city. As we will see, however, these disparities need not preclude a comparative assessment of the six communities.

Earlier gross analyses showed that cases do not exhibit any simple and uniform rise and fall in interaction rates through time.[5] When we shift our attention to individual communities, we similarly find evidence of intracity variability. Among the seven New York City cases, for example, the range in average deviation from an even distribution by quartile extends from 5 per cent to 30 per cent. Corresponding figures for Syracuse are 5 and 22, for Beloit 3 and 24, and for Oberlin 3 and 27. Only the Detroit and Chicago cases, in fact, have deviation ranges consistently below 10 per cent. Despite such temporal variability, though, some trends in interaction frequencies do appear in the six cities. In consonance again with earlier findings,[6] increased communications rates occur in every locale during the fourth quartile. Rises during that period are particularly steep in the two small communities of Beloit and Oberlin. Detroit, to the contrary, exhibits consistent and gradual increases from quartile to quartile, and Chicago, uniform but somewhat sharper increments. Findings of this sort, in fact, portend several other differences discussed below.

An interesting split among the six cities appears when interaction modes—meetings, messages, and public statements—are examined. As Table V.2 indicates, in the three large metropolitan settings of Detroit, New York City, and Syracuse, messages are a more common vehicle of interpersonal decision activity than are meetings. In Beloit and Oberlin, however, the two modes are approximately at parity, and in Chicago, meetings clearly dominate. Public statements distinguish small and large cities even more sharply. Such communications constitute only about 7 per cent of the interactions in both Beloit and Oberlin. In the large city settings, they reach as high as 29 per cent and fall no lower than 16 per

[4] Two of the three Chicago cases describe urban development projects. Two cases on water and sanitation influence the tone of the Syracuse data.

[5] See Tables III.2 and III.3.

[6] Compare Table III.4.

TABLE V.2
Mode Frequencies May Vary Both Between Large and Small Cities and Among Large Ones

	Percentage of Interactions in		
	Meetings	*Messages*	*Public Statements*
Chicago	51	33	16
Detroit	39	42	19
New York City	32	39	29
Syracuse	30	44	26
Beloit	46	47	7
Oberlin	51	42	7

Rows total 100 per cent.

cent. Interaction with larger publics through the mass media is most accentuated in New York City and Syracuse.

PARTICIPANTS IN CITIES

Whatever the effect of issue diversity on frequencies of mode,[7] its impact on the rankings of key actors from city to city is probably greater. The major role of federal officials in Mowitz-Corktown is undoubtedly more a function of an urban renewal issue than a Detroit setting. The activity of religious organizations in Simon-Hospitals reflects the topic of birth control at least as much as it does processes peculiar to New York City. The conspicuous part played by intergovernmental bodies in Banfield-Hall can be traced not only to the characteristic overlay of jurisdictions in Chicago but also to a lakefront location for McCormick Place, requiring the coordinated action of several government agencies. Undoubtedly, the substance of decisions faced by communities drastically alters their casts of participants.

Even this difficulty is not insuperable, for the issue controversies encompassed here have typically engaged a wide range of community interests and, in all but two cities, involve noticeably varied topics. For the same reason, a close (though scarcely complete) similarity obtains in Table V.3 among the six ranks of prominent actors. In each community except Chicago, elected and appointed city officials occupy two of the top three interaction positions. In Chicago, business actors rank first, but they also loom large in nearly every city. They are dominant in Beloit, while in Oberlin and Syracuse they stand second only to elected city

[7] Greater controversiality of issues, for example, probably leads to higher rates of public statements.

TABLE IV.3

Rank Orders of Actor Participants Are Roughly Similar in All Cities

Chicago	*Detroit*	*New York*	*Syracuse*	*Beloit*	*Oberlin*
Business*	Appointed City	Appointed City	Elected City	Business	Elected City
*Ad hoc**	Elected City	Civic	Business	Appointed City	Business
Civic	Appointed County	Elected City	Appointed City*	Elected City	Appointed City
Professional	Business	*Ad hoc*	State*	*Ad hoc*	Professional
Communications	Federal	Business	Professional*	Professional	Federal
Appointed City	State	Communications	Communications	Communications	*Ad hoc*
Elected City	Professional	Professional*	Appointed County	State	State
State	*Ad hoc*	Federal*	Civic*	Civic	Communications
Federal	Communications*	State*	*Ad hoc**	Appointed County*	Appointed County
Appointed County	Civic*	Appointed County	Federal	Federal*	Civic

Ranks are based on total interactions across all the cases in a given city. "Unspecified" and "non-affiliated" actors are omitted. Each column lists in order the ten most overtly participating actor classifications. Adjacent classifications in any column that are followed by an asterisk are tied in rank.

officials. *Ad hoc* and civic groups are most conspicuously active in Chicago and New York City; professional personnel, in Chicago, Syracuse, Beloit, and Oberlin. All three actor categories, however, are numbered among the top ten participants in every city examined. Furthermore, congruity between the communication frequencies of certain actors can be discerned in every city. Thus, the rank attained by business provides a fairly good indicator of the position of professionals. In like manner, the prominence of civic associations furnishes a reasonable index of the activity level of *ad hoc* groups.

Beyond these similarities, Table V.3 also indicates some large differences among the six cities. The Chicago and New York City narratives give evidence of particularly extensive interest group environments. In Detroit, the center stage in decision processes is more frequently occupied by government actors from several levels. The communications industry, apparently important in four communities, is notably less salient in Detroit and Oberlin. In addition, the two small cities are clearly marked off from the four large ones. Indeed, the strength of agreement between actor ranks in Oberlin and Beloit is greater than that between any other pair of cities.[8]

The positions of actor categories in Table V.3 also accord well with many of the interpretations placed on the case material by the authors themselves. For example, Banfield emphasizes that Chicago's highly fragmented formal authority structure leads to policies' and plans' being generated mainly by private organizations with a stake in the outcome. Non-government actors like business, civic associations, professional groups, and newspapers—the Chicago *Tribune* in particular—are credited with especially decisive impacts upon metropolitan decision processes. Only belatedly does the city's elected leadership play an active role in issue controversies, and even then it usually ratifies agreements already reached.[9]

In sharp contrast, Mowitz and Wright see in Detroit a functionally oriented political system, with decision-making largely controlled by powerful government agencies. To be sure, frequent activities by the Board of Commerce and more occasional interventions by *ad hoc* and civic associations do impose some important restraints on government. Furthermore, rivalries among government units in the metropolitan area are prominent and unallayed by any overarching party unification. Despite

[8] The chief variation between these two small communities is in the position of federal officials, with one case, Wildavsky-FAA, accounting for most of this difference.

[9] Edward C. Banfield, *Political Influence* (New York: Free Press, 1961), chs. 8 and 9.

such competition and malintegration, the foci of decision-making remain within the various specialized official bureaucracies.[10]

For their part, Martin, Munger, and associates conclude that Syracuse issue controversies illustrate a highly discontinuous pattern of activities. Though not always of great influence, newspapers and professional personnel are notably frequent participants. Economic organizations, sometimes acting through other community groups, ordinarily lie at the "core of influentials." The case studies also provide evidence for the central position of the Common Council in Syracuse and the Board of Supervisors in Onondaga County. All these actors figure prominently in our analyses, too.[11]

City officials and a co-editor of the local newspaper, according to Wildavsky's detailed analysis, constitute Oberlin's sole general actors. Other participants exhibit considerable issue specialization. Indeed, some can be likened to "meteors," their unprecedented appearance greatly altering the course of a controversy. Furthermore, though specialists can often be aggregated into categories like professional and business, that does not imply they are necessarily united in viewpoint.[12]

As one last illustration, Sayre and Kaufman's *Governing New York City* evaluates participation in a manner quite consonant with our tabular data.[13] They find New York City's fragmented decision-making structure characterized by partially isolated centers, each with consistent, though not entirely exclusive, clienteles. The most notable attribute of the system is its openness:

> No part of the city's large and varied population is alienated from participation in the system. The channels of access to the points of decision are numerous, and most of them are open to any group alert to the opportunities offered and persistent in pursuit of its objectives.[14]

[10] Robert J. Mowitz and Deil S. Wright, *Profile of a Metropolis* (Detroit: Wayne State University Press, 1962), pp. 632–33.
[11] Roscoe C. Martin, Frank J. Munger, *et al., Decisions in Syracuse* (Bloomington: Indiana University Press, 1961), ch. 14. The Republican party, which also receives much attention in this chapter, does not appear as conspicuous in our ranking, but the influence of party is often exerted through other roles in government and business.
[12] Aaron Wildavsky, *Leadership in a Small Town* (Totowa, N. J.: Bedminster Press, 1964), ch. 18. Wildavsky also makes the interesting point that pluralism in Oberlin eventuates in better coordinated policies than pluralism in Chicago, since they are less a product of mere " 'fire trucks' tactics." See p. 344.
[13] Though not a case book, the volume is written by two leading students of urban affairs and the case method. Incidentally, for Beloit, no extensive analyses comparable to those for the other five cities are available.
[14] Wallace S. Sayre and Herbert Kaufman, *Governing New York City* (New York: Russell Sage Foundation, 1960), p. 720.

Sayre and Kaufman also underscore the potential influence of groupings such as civic associations and the press, which are less subject-specific than most interests and therefore more capable of providing some integration among various decision centers. As in Detroit, though, the leading part in issue controversies is played by government officials.[15]

The conclusions of these authors are further corroborated by Table V.4, in which interactions are aggregated into those with government actors only, organized non-government actors only, and both. Except for Oberlin, Chicago exhibits the highest incidence of non-government meetings. Chicago also possesses the second highest rate of meetings between government and non-government and the lowest rate of purely government sessions. Messages follow an almost identical pattern. Finally, the Chicago cases reveal the highest incidence for any city of public statements by non-government actors.

In Detroit, by contrast, more than two-thirds of the meetings are exclusively governmental. In addition, its meetings are lowest in non-government personnel's interacting alone and the second lowest in encounters between government and private interests. The message pattern again closely resembles that of meetings, while on public statements Detroit exhibits the highest rate by government officials and the lowest by persons outside government.

Arrays for New York City and Syracuse generally fall between the extremes of Chicago and Detroit. All three modes indicate rates of exclusive activity by government personnel that are neither as low as Chicago's nor as high as Detroit's. Interactions in Syracuse and New York City that include only representatives of organized non-government similarly occupy an intermediary position. In their frequency of access meetings, however, both cities closely approximate Chicago and markedly exceed Detroit. Furthermore, the access messages in Syracuse and New York City occur at even higher rates.

In general, the distributions for Beloit and Oberlin in Table V.4 resemble those for New York City, but there are some noteworthy exceptions. Access meetings, for example, are extremely infrequent in Oberlin. This is credible in a small community, whose formal organization need not be elaborate and whose key government officials may simultaneously be acting as spokesmen for private interests. This explanation is supported by the finding that more than half the meetings in the Oberlin sample contain solely non-government actors and that *messages* are exchanged between these actors and persons in government at a high frequency.

[15] *Ibid.*, ch. 19.

TABLE V.4

Participation Rates of Actor Combinations Within Cities Follow Several Patterns

	Percentage of Interactions in					
	Chicago	*Detroit*	*New York City*	*Syracuse*	*Beloit*	*Oberlin*
Meetings						
Government only	15	68	32	38	42	37
Organized non-government only	51	7	32	25	30	52
Both	34	22	30	37	25	11
Messages						
Government only	17	61	42	35	50	42
Organized non-government only	44	7	14	13	26	16
Both	39	32	44	52	24	42
Public statements						
Government only	13	54	44	35	33	15
Organized non-government only	84	34	52	60	67	65
Both	3	10	3	3	0	10

Column totals in this table can depart noticeably from 100 per cent because some interactions, e.g., among neighbors, involve neither government personnel nor organized non-government interests.

OTHER INTERACTION ASPECTS IN CITIES

Table V.5 points out that, in general, interactions are more likely to be closed in small cities than in large ones. Nearly 60 per cent of the messages in Beloit and Oberlin are impermeable, while in no other city does the level reach 40 per cent.[16] Moreover, of the large cities, only Chicago exceeds Oberlin or resembles Beloit in its proportion of impermeable meetings. Detroit and Syracuse, which record the lowest rates of closed sessions, concomitantly report the highest incidence of partially open ones, with approximately seven meetings in ten exhibiting partial permeability. In other locales, only four or five meetings in ten lie in this intermediate category.[17] Fully permeable meetings, however, generally occur at similar rates from city to city. Only in New York City, where nearly a fourth of all meetings are wide open, does one find a remarkable difference. Clearly, the magnitude and complexity of organization and procedure in New York City does not preclude plenteous and vocal participation by lay publics and concerned interests.

Large and small cities can also be distinguished by the extent of their formality and informality. As Table V.6 shows, some 36 per cent of messages in Beloit and 44 per cent in Oberlin are informal, while for the metropolitan centers, informal messages range from a low of 6 per cent in Detroit to a high of only 23 per cent in New York City. In meetings, too, Oberlin and Beloit have far higher rates of informality than Detroit and Syracuse. Once again, Chicago deviates considerably from the other large cities. Indeed, its informal meetings occur even more frequently than those in Oberlin. In addition, as a comparison with Table V.4 implies, many of the informal sessions in Chicago are limited to non-government actors. Informal meetings in New York City, by contrast, more often involve government officials, either by themselves or in access encounters with organized interests.

The disparity in meeting informality between Beloit on the one hand and Detroit on the other is remarkable. To appreciate the magnitude of the differences, direct reference to textual descriptions is helpful. The quotations that follow, though not typical of all interactions in the two cities, provide some impression of the contrasting approach to a similar problem about traffic and abutting businesses. Thus, in Beloit:

> A law partner of Blakely called on one of the councilmen, a close friend both socially and politically—the two men also attend the same Beloit

[16] New York City's imposing 38 per cent is certainly influenced by the detailed information furnished about intra- and intergovernmental memoranda in the three Davies cases.

[17] The distributions of partly permeable messages are fairly similar to those for meetings, but at higher levels.

TABLE V.5

Permeability Levels of Meetings and Messages Differentiate the Cities

	Percentage of Interactions in					
	Chicago	*Detroit*	*New York City*	*Syracuse*	*Beloit*	*Oberlin*
Meetings						
Impermeable	46	21	33	24	58	37
Partly permeable	41	70	44	69	36	52
Fully permeable	13	9	23	7	6	11
Messages						
Impermeable	32	18	38	17	58	58
Partly permeable	60	72	53	78	42	40
Fully permeable	8	10	9	5	0	2

TABLE V.6

Informality Is More Typical of the Two Small Communities

	Percentage of Interactions in					
	Chicago	*Detroit*	*New York City*	*Syracuse*	*Beloit*	*Oberlin*
Meetings						
Formal	59	80	65	75	45	64
Informal	41	20	35	25	55	36
Messages						
Formal	86	94	77	85	64	56
Informal	14	6	23	15	36	44

Public statements are omitted from these tables, since by definition they are formal.

> church—and induced the councilman to drive with him through the area around the Corral. While the attorney did not formally ask for a commitment, and none was given, the general nature of his visit was clear.[18]

In Detroit, however:

> Following the formal presentation, a question-and-answer period was held, during which Plan Commission members could be questioned; traffic experts were also on hand to handle technical questions concerning traffic volumes and expressway design.
>
> John Kohl attended a number of meetings and used the question-and-answer period to repeat the by now familiar points in his no-expressway argument.[19]

An examination of continuity levels in Table V.7 uncovers no sharp distinctions—similar to those on permeability and formality—that separate the two small cities and Chicago from the other three large cities. The range for regular meetings in all six cities, for example, extends only from 38 to 50 per cent. Yet within given cities, some interesting patterns can be noted. Consistent with our earlier observations,[20] New York City shows a strikingly high rate of ephemeral meetings. Clearly, its decisional activity is often undertaken by other than habitual participants. Detroit and Syracuse, to the contrary, have low frequencies of ephemeral meetings. Instead, decision-making is focused more exclusively on routine actor networks.

Continuity patterns for meetings provide only a fair index of continuity levels for messages. In Chicago, where interaction regularity infrequently characterizes meetings, there is a similarly low rate for messages. But in New York City, which also has a relatively small proportion of its meetings classified as regular, one finds the second highest percentage of messages with communication lines that predate the controversy. Nonetheless, cities with higher rates of ephemeral meetings tend to exhibit the higher rates of ephemeral messages; cities with few case-patterned meetings usually also have relatively few case-patterned messages, and so on. Indeed, the impression from Table V.7 is that on the attribute "ephemeral," larger cities are divided into two types: those like Chicago and New York City, where novel communications are especially common, and those like Detroit and Syracuse, where interactions more typically flow through established conduits. The findings also suggest the supple adaptability of Chicago's decision structure, the highly bureaucratized patterns of Detroit and Syracuse, and the institu-

[18] Mills-Zoning, p. 26. (Warren E. Mills, Jr., and Harry R. Davis, *Small City Government* [New York: Random House, Inc., 1962]. By permission.)
[19] Mowitz-Expressway, p. 448.
[20] See particularly Table V.5.

TABLE V.7

Most Cities Exhibit Fairly Consistent Continuity Patterns Irrespective of Mode

	Percentage of Interactions in					
	Chicago	*Detroit*	*New York City*	*Syracuse*	*Beloit*	*Oberlin*
Meetings						
Regular	38	50	40	44	48	41
Case patterned	23	29	17	31	22	28
Ephemeral	39	21	43	25	30	31
Messages						
Regular	26	33	42	29	49	22
Case patterned	17	43	28	51	24	41
Ephemeral	57	24	30	20	27	37
Public Statements						
Regular	50	68	71	65	78	50
Case patterned	22	15	6	19	11	15
Ephemeral	28	17	23	16	11	35

tionalized, though interest-responsive, processes in New York City.[21] The supporting data, however, are neither overwhelming nor always consistent, and the similarities in continuity levels among the cities probably deserve equal emphasis.

INTERACTIONS IN ISSUES

The remainder of this chapter focuses upon several issue categories extracted from our larger case sample. It is reasonable to expect that these topics, regardless of locale, will generate characteristic interaction patterns. Indeed, we have already made reference to the strong issue-relatedness of actor participation.[22] Some issues, we may find, are typically low keyed, with a preponderance of formal and partly permeable interactions. Others may be more highly charged, their communications often finding expression in informal and fully permeable settings. Similarly, as the data on continuity should indicate, some issues may frequently require the erection of new decision structures and relationships, while others can ordinarily be accommodated by prevailing institutions and practices.

Table V.8 lists five issue categories, their net interaction totals, and the cases on which they are based. Seven studies that recount decision processes in urban renewal and similar large-scale residential construction are grouped under housing. An adjacent category, urban development, contains six cases on highways, hospitals, civic centers, and port facilities. School integration, as faced in four Northern cities and in New Orleans, comprises another category. The remaining cases in Table V.8 are of wider metropolitan scope: four concern facilities in the related areas of water-sanitation; three others treat determinations of airport location.

None of the five categories evinces any characteristic flow of interactions across quartiles. Each issue domain, in fact, includes narratives with various interaction rates through time. For example, school integration cases overall show a drop in communications after the first quartile and a peak in the last quartile. Yet in Crain-San Francisco the initial period has the most interactions, and in Crain-Buffalo the entire first half is quiescent. There is also considerable variety among housing cases. Some, like Mowitz-Gratiot and Davies-Rockaway, show quite uniform interaction rates; others, like Mowitz-Corktown and Davies-Village, have pronounced clusterings in two of the quartiles. Extensive intra-issue variability of this sort fits well with common sense expectations and pro-

[21] See the citations to Banfield, Mowitz and Wright, Martin, Munger, *et al.*, and Sayre and Kaufman earlier in this chapter. Continuity analysis also reveals Oberlin to be rather like Chicago, and Beloit to be quite different from the other cities.
[22] See the discussion of Table V.3.

vides a further justification for not emphasizing temporal distributions here.[23]

TABLE V.8

Interaction Totals and Case Sources for Five Issue Categories

Issue	*Net Interaction Total*	*Abbreviated Designation of Cases*[a]
Airport location	364	Gladfelter-Airport Mann-Airport Mowitz-Airport
Housing	840	Davies-Rockaway Davies-Village Davies-West Side Mowitz-Corktown Mowitz-Gratiot Muir-Houses Rossi-Hyde Park
School integration	381	Crain-Baltimore Crain-Buffalo Crain-New Orleans Crain-St. Louis Crain-San Francisco
Urban development	532	Altshuler-Hospital Banfield-Hall Banfield-Project Mowitz-Building Mowitz-Expressway Mowitz-Port
Water-Sanitation	288	Gladfelter-Water Herman-Sewage Martin-Water Mowitz-Water

[a] For information on these abbreviated designations see Table III.1 (pp. 22–23).

TABLE V.9

Mode Frequencies Vary Somewhat Among the Issues

	Percentage of Interactions in		
Issue	*Meetings*	*Messages*	*Public Statements*
Airport location	42	33	25
Housing	38	45	17
School integration	44	27	29
Urban development	45	34	21
Water-Sanitation	30	46	24

Rows total 100 per cent.

[23] See note 1, this chapter.

Table V.9 presents data on mode for the issue categories. These aggregate figures, too, may mask considerable variety. For example, though the housing category as a whole has a low proportion of meetings, in three of the narratives—Rossi-Hyde Park, Davies-Village, and Davies-West Side—their rates are reasonably high. Despite such variability, the topics of airport location, school integration, and urban development do exhibit roughly similar mode proportions. Meetings constitute more than four in ten interactions; messages occur less often; and public statements, except in school integration cases, have the least frequency. By contrast, housing cases in Table V.9 show fewer meetings, more frequent messages, and the smallest incidence of communications aimed predominantly at general publics; and water and sanitation cases are marked by even fewer meetings and a great many more messages.

PARTICIPANTS IN ISSUES

Actor participation levels for issues are summarized in Table V.10. Some of the ranks achieved by actor classifications in particular topics are readily comprehended. The direct federal-local relationship in airport location, for example, explains the frequent activity of federal officials, if not their preeminence over other actors. Business' high rank on this topic also seems logical, since the business category includes airlines. Nor is it unanticipated that state, county, suburban, and local intergovernment officials loom large in these cases, since airports are typically at some distance from the central city and government officials from many parts of the metropolitan area are involved. Indeed, only the virtual absence of private actors such as *ad hoc* groups and civic associations[24] should occasion any great surprise.

In housing cases a far more prominent role is assumed by private interests. Eight of the eleven top actors are non-governmental, in contrast with only two in ten for airport location. Moreover, the variety of interest categories is considerable. Included are not only familiar participant classifications like business, *ad hoc,* and civic, but also religion and civil rights, which typically are less prominent. Except for federal personnel, the only noteworthy government actors are appointed and elected city officials. These last two, however, rank first and second in their interaction rates. Housing cases, in short, are intensely local and attract a wide range of a city's organized interests in their determination.

School integration controversies supply perhaps the most predictable complement of participants. School officials, whom we have coded

[24] The participation rates for these categories are too low to qualify them for inclusion in Table V.10.

TABLE V.10

Rank Orders of Actor Participants Are Largely Peculiar to Each Issue

Airport Location	*Housing*	*School Integration*	*Urban Development*	*Water-Sanitation*
Federal	Appointed City	School	Appointed County	Appointed County
Business	Elected City	*Ad hoc*	Business	Elected City
Appointed County	*Ad hoc*	Civil Rights	Elected City	Appointed City
Elected City	Civic	State	Appointed City	Business
State	Business	Court	Intergovernmental	State
Appointed City	Federal	Communications*	State*	Professional
Professional	Professional	Business*	Professional*	Elected County
Intergovernmental	Religion	Civic	Communications	Other Governmental
Elected Suburban	Civil Rights	Elected City	*Ad hoc*	Elected Suburban
Other Governmental	Party*	Professional	Civic	Appointed Suburban
	Communications*			

Ranks are based on total interactions across all the cases on a given issue. "Unspecified" and "non-affiliated" actors are omitted. Each column lists in order the ten most overtly participating actor classifications. Adjacent classifications in any column that are followed by an asterisk are tied in rank.

separately, occupy the first position. The clear presence of *ad hoc,* civil rights, and court personnel is also predictable. Only the like ranking of communications and business, an unusually prominent level for the former and a rather diminished one for the latter, warrants additional comment. The finding is consonant with what is frequently observed in school desegregation controversies: namely, that the local press and television frequently play a critical part in defining events and that business is more chary of entering these conflicts than disputes in which its stakes are more calculable. The actor configuration in school cases, thus, is distinctive and functionally appropriate.

Urban development cases resemble those on housing in their intensive extragovernmental participation. Considerable intervention by business in the physical redevelopment of the central city is apparent, as is the frequent activity of professional, civic, and protest groups. Because their concern is less with urban landscape than with the quality of family life, however, actors representing religious and civil rights interests do not feature in these cases as they do in housing decisions. County, city, state, and local intergovernmental officials, on the contrary, here play quite prominent roles.[25]

Finally, with but two exceptions,[26] issue controversies about water-sanitation have largely governmental casts of actors. Save for federal and out-of-state agencies, every level and agency of government in our code is represented.[27] Participation across government bureaucracies is, of course, indispensable for a problem whose solution so often requires the coordination of many areas and units. Correspondingly, the relative inaction of all organized non-government interests except business is a token of lower public salience for this issue. The area-wide nature of water-sanitation also tends to reduce the impact of many groups organized on a more local basis.

When actor categories are collapsed, as in Table V.11, and communications are classified as wholly governmental, wholly non-governmental, and both, an interesting finding emerges. In all interaction modes, airport location closely resembles water-sanitation. There are also parallel configurations for housing and school integration. Urban development occupies a unique position between the two pairs.

The data seem plausible. Decisions on both airport location and water-sanitation combine a need for extensive technical expertise with a

[25] The preeminence of appointed county officials in cases on urban development can be traced largely to Mowitz-Port. The interaction rate for federal officials is appreciably lower for this issue than for housing, where cases often involve Title I projects.
[26] The professionals, one of these actor categories, are often in contractual relationships with government agencies.
[27] Mowitz-Water even includes officials from Canadian localities.

TABLE V.11

Participation Rates of Actor-Combinations Are Similar for Some Issues, Regardless of Mode

	Percentage of Interactions in				
	Airport Location	*Housing*	*School Integration*	*Urban Development*	*Water-Sanitation*
Meetings					
Government only	66	32	41	57	64
Organized non-government only	9	30	25	17	5
Both	24	30	23	25	30
Messages					
Government only	66	42	42	47	56
Organized non-government only	7	16	14	13	5
Both	27	40	42	40	38
Public statements					
Government only	58	44	38	36	52
Organized non-government only	37	51	49	50	41
Both	4	4	9	12	4

Column totals in this table can depart noticeably from 100 per cent because some interactions, e.g., among neighbors, involve neither government personnel nor organized non-government interests.

need for coordinating several government bureaucracies. Typically, it is from an interplay among government agencies that policies in these fields emerge. While this fact may depress the independent activity of non-governmental actors, their stakes in the decisions are sometimes considerable. As a result, when private interests seek to shape policy, they may interact directly with government personnel. The findings in Table V.11 lend credence to this view: Meetings, messages, and public statements that are completely governmental dominate in the airport and water-sanitation cases. Communications that are wholly non-governmental are relatively scarce, yet the rates of access meetings are not unlike those for the other issues.[28]

Decisions about housing and school integration ordinarily have a more immediate impact on the life styles of local residents. Because of the value choices involved, organized interests are more easily engaged and less likely to defer to government and professional personnel. The narrow focus of these issues, especially housing, also facilitates concerted group activity. Organized interests are able to plan strategies and to convey their demands to the government and more generally to the public

[28] Airport location cases have appreciably low rates of access messages.

at large. Here again, the findings are consonant with our preconceptions. In comparison with water-sanitation and airport location, meetings solely of government personnel in housing and school integration are lower by more than 20 percentage points, while meetings exclusively of organized interests increase by nearly the same proportion. Similar differences occur for messages. There is, in housing and school integration, also a marked rise in the proportion of public statements issued by non-government actors.

Cases dealing with urban development usually involve determinations that are both highly technical and deeply emotional. The design of an expressway requires great expertise, but it can also threaten to disrupt neighborhoods in its path. A civic center is of interest not only to the government agencies that will occupy it but to owners of buildings with which it will compete, to professions that deal with government, and to residents who will be displaced. A new county hospital is similarly of obvious concern to such private actors as doctors, medical schools, and the administrators of private hospitals. It is therefore a reasonable expectation that government will play an exclusive role in urban development decisions less frequently than in airport location and more frequently than in housing. Furthermore, interactions exclusively by non-government interests should also occupy an intermediary position. And both of these tendencies are in fact revealed in Table V.11.

OTHER INTERACTION ASPECTS IN ISSUES

Tables V.12 through V.14 isolate three additional components of interaction. Again we find that the more singularly technical and area-

TABLE V.12
Permeability Levels, Though Varying by Mode, Clearly Distinguish Issues

	Percentage of Interactions in				
	Airport Location	*Housing*	*School Integration*	*Urban Development*	*Water-Sanitation*
Meetings					
Impermeable	33	28	23	28	27
Partly permeable	60	52	42	63	63
Fully permeable	7	20	35	9	10
Messages					
Impermeable	45	24	21	18	9
Partly permeable	44	69	50	68	85
Fully permeable	11	7	29	14	6

Public statements are omitted from this table, since by definition they are fully permeable.

wide issues of airport location and water-sanitation are marked off from the more emotive neighborhood topics of housing and school integration. (The fifth issue domain, urban development, occupies a more variable position.) The descriptions of permeability, formality, and continuity in this section also uncover several noteworthy differences within the two issue pairs.[29]

As Table V.12 shows, decision-making on airport location and water-sanitation features sessions that are partly permeable. Meetings that are neither fully open or closed, a staple of elected government bodies and appointed commissions, also dominate urban development. In addition, more than a quarter of the meetings in these three issue categories are away from the public, while no more than one in ten is wide open. By contrast, housing and school integration show fewer partly permeable meetings and considerably more fully permeable ones. The latter, in the form of mass meetings and demonstrations, are especially common within school integration cases.

Messages generally display permeability levels similar to those for meetings. Partial permeability is very common for water-sanitation and less so for housing and school integration. Entirely open messages are most frequent by far in school integration cases. There are also some curious disparities. For example, messages are rarely closed in water-sanitation cases, although nearly half of them are closed in airport location cases. Similarly, wide open messages are not nearly so frequent in housing controversies as in integration. As a comparison with Table V.9 indicates, these divergent results are not simply a function of the relative frequency of messages. Clearly, though, factors other than a technical-emotional dichotomy are at work here.

On formality, Table V.13 shows a consistent difference between the more exclusively technical issues, where formal meetings and messages most frequently suffice, and the more value-laden issues, where the rate of informal communications increases somewhat. Nevertheless, the distinctions are small and almost completely disappear for messages. In fact, no issue category has as many as two messages in ten behind-the-scenes and informal in tone.

[29] A fourth aspect, spatial location, also deserves brief attention. In general, 85 to 90 per cent of the interactions occur in or near the central city. The sole issue exception is airport location, where fully a third of the interactions take place beyond the metropolitan confines, with equal proportions elsewhere in the state and outside it. In addition, water-sanitation and school integration have more than 10 per cent of their communications locatable in other parts of the state, and housing has more than 5 per cent originating outside the state. Such variations are not to be ignored, but, except for airport location, the fundamental tendency is clearly for localized interaction.

TABLE V.13
Two Issues Show a Greater Frequency of Informal Meetings and Messages

	Percentage of Interactions in				
	Airport Location	*Housing*	*School Integration*	*Urban Development*	*Water-Sanitation*
Meetings					
Formal	75	69	64	74	76
Informal	25	31	36	26	24
Messages					
Formal	87	83	86	92	94
Informal	13	17	14	8	6

Public statements are omitted from this table, since by definition they are formal.

In marked contrast to the continuity findings on cities,[30] those on issues are fairly consistent and meaningful. As Table V.14 indicates, water-sanitation and airport location have the highest frequencies of regular meetings, while school integration and housing have the highest rates of ephemeral meetings. Urban development, in contrast again to the other four issue areas, contains a high proportion of its meetings in networks constructed during the decision process itself.

In general, messages for the issues of airport location and water-sanitation are relatively low in ephemeralness and high in regularity, but

TABLE V.14
Issues Show Small Though Consistent Variations in Their Continuity Levels

	Percentage of Interactions in				
	Airport Location	*Housing*	*School Integration*	*Urban Development*	*Water-Sanitation*
Meetings					
Regular	52	41	45	42	67
Case patterned	20	21	19	34	13
Ephemeral	28	38	36	24	20
Messages					
Regular	34	35	21	31	45
Case patterned	39	37	36	36	32
Ephemeral	27	28	43	33	23
Public statements					
Regular	72	69	67	64	75
Case patterned	15	13	12	13	10
Ephemeral	13	18	21	23	15

[30] See Table V.7.

the contrasts are less clearly drawn than for meetings. Furthermore, there are some sizable disparities between the two issue categories we have considered more value-oriented. School integration, as might be expected from its special cast of participants, frequently involves ephemeral messages. Housing cases, to the contrary, contain many regular messages, largely in the form of governmental staff memoranda.[31] In addition, all five issues have about the same rates of case-patterned messages.

As in our full sample of cases,[32] public statements in each issue area emanate mainly from habitual sources like government officials, the press, and chambers of commerce. Even so, a persistent if slim distinction between the more exclusively technical and the more completely emotive issues can be perceived. Thus, a larger proportion of public announcements in airport location and water-sanitation cases follow regular networks, and a smaller proportion are ephemeral. Even though the differences are not sharp, their direction is consistent.

These data on continuity lead us to the conclusion that, regardless of locale, the five issue categories bear different relationships to decision structures. Questions about water and sanitation, and to a lesser extent about the location of airports, are more easily contained within prevailing decisional channels. Undoubtedly, this fact is explained both by the government's near monopoly of technical expertise and by the infrequency of challenge from potentially competing structures in the communities. Housing and school integration, the latter in particular, illustrate decision processes that adhere far less to established networks. In contrast to the other three issues, direct encounters in these topics seem especially unpredictable. Urban development, our last issue category, though not easily accommodated by on-going decision patterns, is not characterized by idiosyncratic interaction either. Instead, especially at meetings, it tends to produce and sustain new decision networks.

PROPOSITIONAL SUMMMARY

The data on interactions in six cities and on five issues offer firmest support for the following generalizations.

1. Despite considerable variability within each city, interaction rates characteristically show increases in the fourth quartile.
2. Public statements occur less frequently in small cities than in large ones.

[31] As noted before, the three New York City housing cases—Davies-Rockaway, Davies-Village, and Davies-West Side—contain many citations to documents that circulated within and between government agencies.
[32] See Table IV.12.

3. Government actors are especially prominent in Detroit's issue controversies; organized non-government interests, in Chicago's and New York City's.
4. In every city except New York, business actors rank first among non-government participants.
5. The actor rank orders in the two small communities, Beloit and Oberlin, correspond more closely than those in any other pairs of cities.
6. Access meetings appear at a lower rate in Detroit than in other major cities, but the rate in Oberlin is lower still.
7. Fully permeable meetings occur most frequently in New York City, and impermeable meetings in Chicago and the two small cities; by contrast, partial permeability overwhelmingly characterizes Detroit and Syracuse.
8. Informal interactions are most typical of the small communities, Beloit and Oberlin, and of Chicago.
9. In Chicago and New York City, ephemeral communications are especially common, whereas in Detroit and Syracuse, interactions tend to follow established networks.
10. Chicago clearly departs from patterns found in other major cities in its lesser participation by government officials, fewer exclusively government interactions, higher rates of impermeability, more frequent informality, and consistently lower incidence of regularity.
11. Messages are most prevalent in cases on housing and water-sanitation; meetings similarly predominate in cases on airport location, school integration, and urban development.
12. Housing attracts the widest range of non-government interests; water-sanitation, the narrowest range.
13. Although the central city alone supplies most of the government officials who are frequent participants in housing decisions, personnel from several jurisdictions are frequently conspicuous in cases on airport location and water-sanitation.
14. Representatives of business, prominent in all five issue areas, are least visible in school integration controversies.
15. Interactions exclusively among government personnel are most characteristic of airport and water-sanitation decisions; housing and school integration issues, in contrast, show the highest proportions of exclusively non-government interactions.
16. Fully permeable meetings occur with unusual frequency in cases about housing and school integration, while partial permeability is especially common in the other three issues.

17. Although formality is a dominant attribute in all five issue areas, it particularly characterizes airport location and water-sanitation cases.
18. Meetings and messages are notably ephemeral in controversies about school integration and housing and notably regular in those about water-sanitation and airport location.
19. The highest proportion of case-patterned meetings occurs in urban development cases.
20. On various interaction aspects, water-sanitation narratives closely resemble those on airport location, and housing narratives, those on school integration; cases dealing with urban development, however, exhibit features of both these pairs.

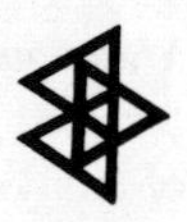

CHAPTER VI

Some Implications and Applications

WE NOW EXPLORE three problems that have been suggested, but not confronted, in our previous discussions. How adequate, we shall ask, are our procedures? What is their theoretical relevance? And can we demonstrate, more directly than we have thus far, their disciplinary utility? The last of these questions is examined at greatest length, while the first is treated with relative brevity; and that, we believe, is as it should be. For while it is interesting to know that certain things can be done and that doing them seems to matter, a more crucial issue is whether or not their achievement has any demonstrable applications.

Our consideration of methodological adequacy leads us to reappraise both the analytic categories employed in this volume and the available case materials on which they rest. While some refinements might even now be introduced into our code, several new strategies in the preparation of case studies are more likely to further the process analyses begun here. To this end we offer case writers a few modest proposals about the quality and quantity of narratives.

In evaluating the theoretical implications of our approach, we avoid defending the intrinsic importance of an interaction emphasis—hopefully the justifications in Chapter II have allayed most doubts on this score—and instead consider the fit between our methods and more customary ways of studying community politics. It is our intention to show that alternate perspectives like power, ideology, and institutions are not rivals of an interaction approach; that, indeed, each of them can be restated in largely interactional terms. At the same time, however, these other lines of analysis do differ so radically from the framework of inquiry employed here, both in their subjective components and in the objective data they ordinarily examine, that it seems appropriate to apply interactional analysis to each of them separately. Such a procedure should also increase our appreciation of the phenomena associated with various institutions, ideologies, and distributions of power.

In assessing the disciplinary worth of our data, we probe more closely the way in which our interaction categories help in amplifying these three familiar political emphases. Here, as before, we can be only suggestive, since a full demonstration of the relevance of our findings would require much additional research and another book. We confine ourselves, therefore, merely to sketching a few of the applications to which our materials might be put. In particular, we illustrate how interaction data can add a valuable process dimension to a description of reform institutions in American cities, a classification of communities according to their predominant political norms, and an account of power configurations in urban politics. Insofar as these more usual categories of political research are shown associated with recognizable interaction patterns, we shall have attained our objectives.

This brief inquiry into the methodological, theoretical, and disciplinary merit of our procedures and findings is designed for those readers who, like us, have been all too aware that the previous discussions have skirted many themes customary in studies of community politics. In the main, we have used cases to burnish previously unattended interaction facets of the decision process. Now they, by reflection, can help illumine more sharply topics long at the center of political analyses.

METHODOLOGICAL ADEQUACY

Nearly all our efforts in the preceding chapters have been directed to a description and classification of interactions associated with decision-making. Both the broader outlines of interactivity and many of its finer components have concerned us. Our accounts have emphasized the manner of transmission, participants, temporal position, spatial location, diffusion, tone, and stability of networks. The contributions of these interaction aspects to the decision process have been analyzed both separately and in various combinations. We have also sought to isolate distinctive patterns in given locales and issue areas.[1]

Unencumbered by practical problems for the moment, we can easily imagine improvements in our coding procedures. Some refinements involve only further specifications within the categories we presently em-

[1] See, respectively, Chapters III, IV, and V.

ploy. For example, there is obvious value in a more detailed classification of participant roles, since internal heterogeneity would be reduced.[2] If sufficient detail is introduced, it should also become possible to uncover the existence of interacting cliques and constellations.[3] Other changes might involve the recognition of additional aspects of interaction, by assessing, for example, the affective-informational balance of communications or the extent of agreement in which they culminate. Our failure to adopt these categories and classifications in our analysis stems only from operational considerations. An evaluation of permeability levels seemed far easier than an identification of emotive qualities. Similarly, a division of temporal flows into four quartiles rather than, say, ten deciles appeared sensible, especially given the frequent imprecisions in interaction dating.

Lack of clarity in the descriptions of events presently poses, in fact, the most serious obstacle to a systematic treatment of cases. Fortunately, this difficulty can in the future be overcome without altering the basic design of narratives. Case writers probably need do little more than employ interaction as their analytic unit and adopt some common framework of categories like those described in this book. It is not necessary for them to become scribes, attempting futilely to record everything: indeed, to employ that strategy would be to abandon the application of intelligent selectivity, which as social scientists they bring to their task. Nor do they have to come to any agreements with their fellow investigators about fundamental theoretical perspectives. About all that is asked of case authors is that they take greater care in dating communications, strive to identify the participants in interactions more accurately, and be more informative about the context of activities so that characteristics like permeability and formality can be studied readily.[4]

Yet if all 32 cases in our sample met these criteria—and a few now approach them—we would still be constrained to employ a fairly modest

[2] At present, the classification business includes a neighborhood merchant as well as the Chamber of Commerce, while *ad hoc* encompasses front organizations for business, evanescent associations of local property owners, and newly emergent societies to preserve school segregation.

[3] On cliques (or "crowds," as they seem to be styled in Atlanta), see Floyd Hunter, *Community Power Structure* (Chapel Hill: University of North Carolina Press, 1953), ch. 3. On constellations see William L. C. Wheaton, "Integration at the Urban Level," in Philip E. Jacob and James V. Toscano, eds., *The Integration of Political Communities* (Philadelphia: Lippincott, 1964), pp. 120–42.

[4] Such self-conscious exactitude in handling communications data should not greatly change the format of cases or undermine their pedagogic and illustrative utility; moreover, if the alterations do seem detrimental to these ends, it would still be possible for case writers to produce two drafts of their work—one designed, as today, for general purposes, while the other more detailed version furnishes a basis for systematic analysis.

interpretive instrument. For though at times some 2,842 interactions have been available for analysis,[5] the sample is still much smaller than we could have used. Even its considerable size rapidly becomes insufficient when several controls are employed at once. In Table IV.6, for example, where the data are simultaneously divided into three modes, four quartiles, three actor combinations, and three continuity levels, the 108 resultant cells push the information supply nearly to its limits.[6]

Clearly, the analyses would benefit from considerably larger pools of interaction data. This assertion scarcely conflicts with the claim by critics of case studies that a piling of narrative upon narrative is ill suited to the testing of carefully drawn hypotheses,[7] for most critics (and advocates) of cases have been thinking of them as total entities rather than as sources of micro units. This molar predilection also helps explain the recent proposals that cases be written for assemblage into preselected "clusters." The strategy, it was believed, would reduce intercase variability and foster comparisons. There was from the first, however, much reason to doubt that the results could be conceptually meaningful.[8] Furthermore, any substantive comparability attained among the cases is bought at the price of severely limiting the number of narratives available for analysis.[9]

Our proposal is not for more superficially similar cases but simply for more extensive arrays of interaction data through cases. Consequently,

[5] This is true in most of Chapter IV. In Chapter V sample sizes are smaller, because the data are restricted to particular issues and locales. Our units of analysis are still fewer in Chapter III, since case quartiles furnish the basis for computation.

[6] When only subsamples are relevant, as in Table IV.16, the data are depleted much more rapidly.

[7] See especially Herbert Kaufman, "The Next Step in Case Studies," *Public Administration Review,* 18 (1958), 52–59. Kaufman remarks, for example (p. 56), that "new cases do not add to what the earlier ones taught us, for the common denominator appears and reappears in each story."

[8] "However, what the cases in each cluster will share with their fellows is a concentration on areas of governmental operation rather than convergence on specific propositions whose validity is being investigated. . . . These seem to be so broad that the results will not be significantly different from what has been done thus far. . . ." *Ibid.,* p. 59. For an example of what clustering has produced see Edwin A. Bock, ed., *Government Regulation of Business* (New York: Prentice-Hall, 1965). Its 7 cases range from "The Great Cranberry Crisis" and "The Battery Additive Controversy" to "The Emergency Oil Lift to Europe in the Suez Crisis." Bock (*ibid.,* pp. vii–viii) specifies some 11 perspectives that 2 or more of these cases feature; but only one of the 11—"regulated firms or industries"—involves as many as 6 cases, and that theme is virtually implicated in the title of the book.

[9] Frederick C. Mosher, ed., *Governmental Reorganizations* (Indianapolis: Bobbs-Merrill, 1967), comes much closer to what Kaufman deems desirable (*op. cit.,* p. 57), since it is built around a fairly clear theoretical proposition, namely, the participation hypothesis. Because Mosher uses the 12 cases in his volume as his basic analytic units, however, even he is limited generally in his schematic interpretations to qualitative and impressionistic ratings.

there is no need for restrictions on subject matter. Indeed, a mixed lot may lead more readily to a comprehensive understanding of decisional patterns than would a set of narrowly premised parallel accounts. To be sure, several case studies focusing on a single city or issue would ease the analyst's job, but every competently executed case can provide grist for theoretical mills by permitting more sophisticated and multivariate analysis. In this respect, studies that represent "targets-of-opportunity"[10] are as valuable as those in preordained clusters. Both kinds encourage further specifying and concretizing of the interactions that underpin politics.

Our advice to case writers, then, is simple and direct. Doubtless, they could compose their narratives more consistently and explicitly, just as our code could undoubtedly be refined and extended. The crucial requirement, however, is that there be more cases, so that more complex and probing investigations of interactions can be undertaken. Whether or not the cases proceed from some already agreed upon topical or propositional concern is unrelated to this end. By measurably increasing the fund of communications open to scrutiny, they will all aid us in comprehending the many aspects of decision processes in metropolises and elsewhere.

THEORETICAL RELEVANCE

A nearly exclusive emphasis upon interactions might initially seem open to criticism for its neglect of other crucial components of community decision-making. Should not our inquiries also have considered distributions of influence, impacts of ideology, and constraints imposed by institutional structures? These familiar perspectives surely hold more promise for the political analyst than the behavioral unit represented by interactions.[11]

The objection, though, is perhaps less substantive than it initially appears, for the competing perspectives can themselves be translated into the language of interaction and communication. Thus, an institution can be viewed as a stable set of interpersonal behavior. Lasswell and Kaplan, for example, define it as "a pattern composed of culture traits specializing to the shaping and distribution of a particular value (or set of values)," a culture trait in turn being "an act characteristic of a group," as evidenced in personality traits, group acts, and "other interpersonal practices."[12] Sufficiently close observation makes it possible to identify these

[10] Mosher, *op. cit.,* p. xi.

[11] Compare Macridis' suggestively ecumenical attitude toward comparative politics, which touches on all four approaches. Roy C. Macridis, *The Study of Comparative Government* (Garden City, N. Y.: Doubleday, 1955), chs. 3–9.

[12] Harold D. Lasswell and Abraham Kaplan, *Power and Society* (New Haven: Yale University Press, 1950), p. 47.

persistent structures of activity and demeanor and to assess the interplay between such institutionalized performances and other behaviors that impinge more evanescently upon them.[13] Furthermore, the actuality of legal systems can be ascertained in just the same manner.[14]

Similarly, ideologies can be recognized not merely in the pronouncements of professional ideologues and the texts of received scripture but in the implications of observable interactions.

> Rival ideologies exist side by side within the non-authoritarian community and try to assert their own superiority; the groups identified with each ideology in fact struggle for supremacy or at least toleration. . . . In each case this expression of group interest merely gives formal content to the body of values believed in by the group. Thus values and interests are the internal and external aspects of a given group ideology.[15]

To illustrate, are interactions often secret and informal? If so, that is a fact of ideological relevance even if the governing myth in the community proclaims a democratic equality of access and open policies openly achieved.[16] Are businessmen frequent participants at crucial meetings and religious representatives usually absent from them? Probably these behavioral differences indicate the domination of a business ethic and the relative decline of a sectarian one. Does business often avoid civil rights issues and other touchy problems that appear devoid of tangible gains? Very likely that betokens the shallowness of such value theories as "welfare capitalism."[17]

[13] Erving Goffman, "The Nature of Deference and Demeanor," *American Anthropologist,* 58 (1956), 473–502, shows how far an observational strategy can proceed in this direction.

[14] "The conjunction of common expectations concerning authority with a high degree of corroboration in actual operation is what we understand by law." Myres S. McDougal and Harold D. Lasswell, "The Identification and Appraisal of Diverse Systems of Public Order," *American Journal of International Law,* 53 (1959), 9. Our own practice of coding sessions and internal communiques of preexisting organizations as regular in continuity proceeds from the same logic, for regularity is clearly a hallmark of a community's institutions.

[15] Ernst B. Haas and Allen S. Whiting, *Dynamics of International Relations* (New York: McGraw-Hill, 1956), pp. 26–27 (italics omitted).

[16] The governing myth, "exoterically" available to a wide audience, is sometimes supplemented by an "esoteric" analysis known only to the elite few. See Gabriel A. Almond, *The Appeals of Communism* (Princeton: Princeton University Press, 1954), ch. 3.

[17] A good statement of the "welfare capitalism" orientation occurs in Russell Davenport, "The Greatest Opportunity on Earth," *Fortune,* 40 (1949), 65 ff. Recent studies of the actual behavior of businessmen, however, show that many of them do not see any appreciable advantages from intervention even on a topic like tariffs, which most of us would consider of undeniable economic importance. See especially Raymond A. Bauer, Ithiel de Sola Pool, and Lewis A. Dexter, *American Business and Public Policy* (New York: Atherton, 1963), parts 2 and 3.

Many notions about power can also be restated in interaction and communication terms.[18] A participant may be rated powerful if a systematic tracing of message flows indicates his centrality in a communications network. He may also seem powerful because of early or frequent participation, because many remarks by others are addressed to him, or because he often receives inquiries of particular sorts, e.g., requests for information, suggestion, or permission.[19] Other interactional measures of power include being on the ultimately "winning" side or being present in settings that are deemed to matter most.[20]

Conceptualizations of power, ideology, and institutions in behavioral terms are, therefore, not theoretically implausible. They appear, however, to have two drawbacks. First, their techniques are unduly laborious, especially given the easier methods at hand. Second and more importantly, they almost surely fail to seize upon many crucial components of their phenomena.

To rely upon repetitive combinations of interaction alone in defining institutions is to be unnecessarily devious. Political science has long possessed simpler and more direct methods for their identification and description: indeed, a familiar complaint against the discipline charges that it is too institutionally descriptive and structurally static.[21] In addition, much relevant data about formal political institutions can be found in standard reference sources. There one may learn how the city council is elected, in what fields semi-autonomous commissions operate, under what circumstances bond elections are required, and so on. Many other institutions in a city, such as its leading corporations, civic associations, and churches, are similarly set forth in various official and even popular compilations.

Often, too, sources other than interaction compendia seem more relevant to an initial comprehension of ideology and power. Statements and manifestos by officials and by private notables do often reflect the stan-

[18] Compare Karl W. Deutsch, *The Nerves of Government* (New York: Free Press, 1963), ch. 7.

[19] Indicators like these, which apparently tap more than a single dimension, are quite prominent in small group research concerned with leadership. An informed discussion can be found in Sidney Verba, *Small Groups and Political Behavior* (Princeton: Princeton University Press, 1961), chs. 5–8.

[20] The first criterion is pivotal in many studies of voting by judges and legislators. An excellent example is Robert A. Dahl, "The Concept of Power," *Behavioral Science*, 2 (1957), 201–15. The second standard is often used as a check on otherwise derived power rankings in local communities. See, for example, Floyd Hunter, Ruth C. Schaffer, and Cecil G. Sheps, *Community Organization* (Chapel Hill: University of North Carolina Press, 1956), ch. 7.

[21] See Macridis, *op. cit.*, chs. 1 and 2, Gabriel A. Almond and G. Bingham Powell, Jr., *Comparative Politics* (Boston: Little, Brown, 1966), pp. 1–3, and (for a close focus upon municipal studies) Lawrence J. R. Herson, "The Lost World of Municipal Government," *American Political Science Review*, 51 (1957), 330–45.

dards, outlooks, and norms brought to bear upon political choices, and the materials are already there for the studying.[22] Also, a reputational approach supplies a quick means of determining the persons who are *thought* to have influence in a community. Such findings often correlate reasonably well with other indices of power, and they are not irrelevant to the actual power positions of individuals either.[23]

Not only do easier methods exist for estimating power and identifying ideologies and institutions than an observation of interaction regularities, the three topics involve more than directly viewable extra-organic behavior. Indeed, they are thoroughly pervaded by feelings.[24] Subjective, orientational, reflective, attitudinal attributes unquestionably adhere to them, making impossible their adequate description merely through direct recordings of interpersonal activity.

Power, for example, encompasses not only role performances and other directly viewable phenomena. It also includes the status accorded performers by significant others. Besides pervading active "clearances" with those who supposedly matter, it is implicated whenever anyone's opinions are taken into consideration, even if he has done nothing at all. Power distributions may be revealed, in fact, not so much in decisions that are reached as in non-decisions that are not raised at all.[25]

In like manner, ideologies and institutions also have their orientational aspects. Although these are most salient perhaps among the former, they are certainly not absent from the latter. To the contrary, as Turner and Killian remark:

> Institutional behavior characterizes groups which are envisaged in and guided by the culture of the larger society. Accordingly, institutional behavior refers to activities which are necessary to the conduct of society's business, which support the norms of the larger society.[26]

The main thrust of our argument is this. Many characteristics ordinarily subsumed under topics like power, ideology, and institutions can

[22] One good way of employing them is through systematically insightful content analysis. A fine example at the local level is Anselm L. Strauss, *Images of the American City* (New York: Free Press, 1961).
[23] See Harry Scoble, "Leadership Hierarchies and Political Issues in a New England Town," in Morris Janowitz, ed., *Community Political Systems* (New York: Free Press, 1961), pp. 117–45, and M. Kent Jennings, *Community Influentials* (New York: Free Press, 1964).
[24] Compare Susanne K. Langer's comments about purely behavioral psychology in her treatise *Mind* (Baltimore: Johns Hopkins University Press, 1967), especially ch. 2.
[25] Peter Bachrach and Morton S. Baratz, "Decisions and Nondecisions," *American Political Science Review*, 57 (1963), 632–42.
[26] Ralph H. Turner and Lewis M. Killian, *Collective Behavior* (Englewood Cliffs, N. J.: Prentice-Hall, 1957), p. 12.

be expressed in interactional terms. Research based solely on these translations, however, would be unnecessarily costly and would scant many obvious sources of information. Furthermore, it would neglect non-behavioral, though actual, subjective components. A better strategy limits interaction analysis to *descriptions of process*—a restriction that scarcely reduces its usefulness in political research.

INTERACTION AND THE REFORM PACKAGE

This section and the next two apply the analytic categories introduced by our study to classifications already in the lexicons of most political scientists. We will illustrate how our approach can amplify these familiar concept sets, each of which bears directly on decision-making in American cities. First, we examine some behavioral implications of "good government" institutions. Later, we apply a similar interaction analysis to Williams and Adrian's typology of community political norms and to the range of community power structures delineated by Rossi.[27] All three discussions will extract process notions embedded in these themes and indicate, through a series of hypotheses, how interaction data can facilitate their empirical testing and help make research on decision styles an integral part of political analysis.

The term "reform package" is an omnibus phrase that typically includes such components as non-partisan election, council-manager government, and at-large representation. Each of these political structures was first introduced early in this century by middle-class civic reformers, whose influence is still felt in the reshaping of municipal institutions. The constant aim of their crusade has been to eliminate the inefficiency and corruption of political middlemen, most notably the partisan politicians, so that the real needs of a "virtuous" citizenry might be heard and a corps of administrative specialists might be empowered to serve them.[28]

Contemporary appraisals of reform structures tend to dwell less upon actual performance than upon certain political implications. A reasonably wide consensus holds that most reform institutions have administratively fulfilled their original objectives. There is far more disagreement about the legitimate role of managers, the political content of most community decisions, the effects of non-partisanship upon local leadership recruit-

[27] Oliver P. Williams and Charles R. Adrian, *Four Cities* (Philadelphia: University of Pennsylvania Press, 1963), Peter H. Rossi, "Power and Community Structure," *Midwest Journal of Political Science*, 4 (1960), 390–401.

[28] For a useful summary of reform ideals and experiences, see Edward C. Banfield and James Q. Wilson, *City Politics* (Cambridge: Harvard University Press, 1963), chs. 11–13.

ment, and the implications of reform for state or national party activities.[29]

Given these emphases, it may seem curious that empirical research contrasting policy outputs in reform and non-reform cities has been so scarce.[30] Yet the difficulties in analysis make the dearth understandable. What classification, for example, should be assigned cities whose institutions are only nominally reformed? Chicago's "non-partisan" city council furnishes an obvious example. Nor have reform cities invariably accepted every item in the "good government" package. In addition, because cities most receptive to such reform institutions as the manager plan apparently differ in several respects from localities that avoid it, it is imperative for studies to introduce many simultaneous demographic controls.[31] Finally, if the two types of municipal structures mainly reflect pervasive political ethics, as some observers contend, it would perhaps be wiser to trace both institutional and policy differences to the same enveloping political culture.[32]

Yet, even if no major policy differences were discernible between reform and non-reform cities—a finding that might stem from a nationwide similarity in urban exigencies—their means of arriving at community decisions still might be dissimilar. In raising this point, we need not be too concerned that the institutions do not alone contribute to the different patterns. It is of greater interest that the forces predisposing cities to adopt or reject the structural innovations probably induce characteristic varieties of decision-making observable in case narratives.

What suggestions, then, are there in commentaries about reformed

[29] Two leading studies in this genre, both by Charles R. Adrian, are "A Study of Three Communities," *Public Administration Review,* 18 (1958), 208–13, and "Some General Characteristics of Nonpartisan Elections," *American Political Science Review,* 46 (1952), 766–76. Compare also Karl A. Bosworth, "The Manager *Is* a Politician," *Public Administration Review,* 18 (1958), 216–22.

[30] For an able start at filling this gap, see Robert L. Lineberry and Edmund P. Fowler, "Reformism and Public Policies in American Cities," *American Political Science Review,* 61 (1967), 701–16.

[31] Except on religion and ethnicity, Lineberry and Fowler do not uncover any strong demographic differences between cities with and without reformed structures. Kessel, however, in examining the adoption of the manager plan, finds several significant differences between cities that have employed this one specific reform and those that have not. John H. Kessel, "Governmental Structure and Political Environment," *American Political Science Review,* 56 (1962), 615–20. A similar finding for a large sample of suburban communities is reported in Leo F. Schnore and Robert R. Alford, "Forms of Government and Socio-Economic Characteristics of Suburbs," *Administrative Science Quarterly,* 8 (1963), 1–17.

[32] A good example of this approach is James Q. Wilson and Edward C. Banfield, "Public-Regardingness as a Value Premise in Voting Behavior," *American Political Science Review,* 58 (1964), 876–87. For a later study that casts some doubt on their conclusions, see Raymond E. Wolfinger and John O. Field, "Political Ethos and the Structure of City Government," *American Political Science Review,* 60 (1966), 306–26, particularly 321–24.

cities that would imply certain more or less distinctively shaped processes? Quite clearly, reform institutions were intended to adjust vectors of influence in urban decision-making. Access by some sectors of the community is increased, frequently at the expense of others. In theory, at least, the impact of nationally affiliated partisan organizations is totally eliminated. The preponderance of political influence in the city shifts from elected officials and from such partial interests as social and economic minorities to professional administrators and more community-wide interests. The change, according to Sayre and Kaufman, is "to the 'politics' of strategically located interest groups, or organized bureaucracies, or autonomy-minded appointed executives, or some alliance of these three types."[33]

The governance of reform cities supposedly accords with good business management practices. Officials are guided by standards of efficiency and economy rather than by calculations of group strengths. High administrative offices in the city are available to persons from the outside or to local residents whose inculcated occupational values make their outlook cosmopolitan. All the same, the new institutions are not intended to be any less effective and responsible agencies of a true popular will. Instead, by weakening and eliminating patterns of practice that lend influence to more parochial interests, the reform structures supposedly insure a fashioning of policies appropriate to the needs of the community in its entirety.

Isolation of government policy-makers from particularistic pressures and unprofessional demands probably results in the depersonalization of relationships between constituents and public officials. As Banfield and Wilson write:

> Generally speaking, the only contact between the voters and the nonpartisan official is through the ballot box. There is no party headquarters, no precinct organization, and no ward office to provide a basis of informal contact at the neighborhood level.[34]

The lines of communication, often reaching immediately to the city manager, his key aides, and the elected council, tend to become formalized and routinized. Longer incumbencies of decision-makers also can increase communications stability.

Where reform has been introduced, decisions are usually made either within the governmental core by an impersonal, "non-political" bureauc-

[33] Wallace S. Sayre and Herbert Kaufman, *Governing New York City* (New York: Russell Sage Foundation, 1960), p. 733. Descriptions of reform in New York City refer to its occasional fusion administrations rather than to any specific sets of institutions, but the consequences of the movement in New York City do not seem unlike those elsewhere.

[34] Banfield and Wilson, *op. cit.*, p. 161.

racy or at the "periphery of the system"—for example, by civic and business leaders.[35] In either event, the decision style is typically one of relatively low intensity. As Adrian, among others, has suggested, non-partisan cities apparently avoid highly controversial and threatening issues whenever possible. In fact, considerable effort is frequently expended to insure that decision-making appears routine,[36] for in reformed cities, strong issue conflicts are ordinarily interpreted as serious threats to the political health of the entire community.

These brief observations about the reform package, most of them unavoidably general, suggest a number of hypotheses that may be expressed in the categories applied in our earlier interaction analyses. Overall, the following tendencies are more likely to be characteristic of cities with reform institutions than of those that have retained older forms.

1. Interaction rates should vary rather little across the time span of an issue. Processes in a decision controversy should not show alternating excitations and relaxations, nor should interactions strongly cluster in the final quartile.
2. Public statements are likely to occur at somewhat diminished rates, while messages appear at fairly high frequencies.
3. Recurring participant constellations in narratives probably reflect the "good government" alliances prevalent in the community. These dominant coalitions should be especially prominent in initiating message inputs for their cities. (N.B. While clear differences should appear when the dominant actor casts in reform and non-reform cities are contrasted, the reform category will itself exhibit considerable heterogeneity, both because its advocates vary from place to place and because some reformed locales have been more successful than others in reducing the impact of "old-line" groups.)
4. Communications between government officials in the central city and those outside it should occur early and often in many narratives, for directly partisan clashes are obviated and, besides, many officials in reformed cities are oriented to extra-local cues.
5. Interactions probably take place with least frequency in wide open settings, and only slightly more often completely outside the public purview. Instead, their rate of partial permeability should be conspicuously high.
6. Formal communications should strongly predominate over informal ones.

[35] Lineberry and Fowler, *op. cit.*, p. 716.
[36] Adrian, "A Study of Three Communities," p. 213.

7. The routinization of issue controversies likely eventuates in a high proportion of interactions following networks that predate given cases. Ephemeral interactions, in contrast, should be quite rare. Case-patterned communications probably do not differ greatly in total frequency, though more of them perhaps are restricted to participants functionally related to the topics under consideration. All three kinds of interaction continuity should be characterized, furthermore, by rather low emotive levels.

INTERACTION AND COMMUNITY NORMS

Another illustration of the amplifying effect interaction data have for political concepts may be drawn from Williams and Adrian's typology of dominant community norms.[37] Their studies of four middle-size cities lead them to posit four varieties of role perceptions residents have of their local government: as a promoter of economic growth, as a provider of amenities, as a "caretaker," or as an arbiter of competing interests. These images in turn offer an index to local policy orientations and the aims of decisional institutions. Though no setting seems exclusively devoted to just one of these norms, some are plainly more dominant than others.[38]

Our brief description of each type stresses those elements that bear particularly on decision activities. Admittedly, three of the four classifications apparently do not revolve about considerations of process: instead, promoting growth, providing amenities, and acting as caretaker all ostensibly focus upon the substance of decisions. Only the arbiter theme is clearly concerned with how decisions are made. Nonetheless, it seems probable that communities with dissimilar emphases of role and policy will also exhibit contrasting decision styles. Such patterns of interaction, moreover, should pervade many substantive areas in a city and not just those that provide its normative keynote.

The role perceptions described by Williams and Adrian are surely not distributed at random in American cities. For example, arbiter themes are a more common feature of large, heterogeneous communities, while caretaker norms likely predominate in small, homogeneous cities. Simi-

[37] Williams and Adrian, *op. cit.,* especially pp. 21–36. The same typology appears in an earlier article by Williams alone. See Oliver P. Williams, "A Typology for Comparative Local Government," *Midwest Journal of Political Science,* 5 (1961), 150–64.
[38] Another notable study of local communities that heavily emphasizes role perceptions is Robert E. Agger, Daniel Goldrich, and Bert E. Swanson, *The Rulers and the Ruled* (New York: Wiley, 1964). The book stresses throughout "shifts in the scope of government," a notion that also seems to underlie the Williams and Adrian analyses.

larly, the two remaining types seem more prominent in affluent residential suburbs. A focus on amenities or on growth, as the authors indicate, is also especially compatible with municipal reform institutions. Still, the four orientations cannot be explained in wholly structural terms: even cities that are institutionally or demographically similar are capable of quite different norms and policy directions.

Our interest here is not in establishing any independent causal relationships or in demonstrating the adequacy of the classifications. For our purposes it is sufficient merely that the normative typology usefully distinguish constraining community values about decision-making. We can then more fully develop these categories by underscoring their interactional component, thereby also permitting their use as frameworks for process analysis.

In the first of the types described by Williams and Adrian, "the promotion of economic growth," a community is permeated by a booster spirit. Its political institutions are delegated major responsibility for fostering programs aimed at increasing local economic resources by attracting new industries and nurturing old ones. To this end, decision-makers usually require considerable authority, expertise, and coordination. The leadership structure includes a professional bureaucracy that works in cooperation with top business leaders, often in the chamber of commerce, and with various civic associations. Those making policy are also frequently obliged to work closely with government officials in adjoining jurisdictions in order to accommodate fully the industries they seek to retain or recruit.

Although there is no one strategy uniquely conducive to economic growth, community decisions are often largely negative in this climate oriented to the producer. The city fathers are anxious that nothing be done to jeopardize the locale's growth or tarnish its good reputation. The result is a brand of politics that is markedly restrained.[39]

A second urban milieu works largely toward "providing and securing life's amenities." A high value is placed on maintaining the community's character and keeping its level of services high. Leadership is expected to satisfy residents as consumers rather than to provide environments suited to a few producers, a choice that is made feasible by the relative economic prosperity of the city's population and its general consensus about life style. Similarly, those in elected and appointed positions possess a fairly well-articulated and consonant set of policy standards.

Under these conditions, government officials, and especially the permanent bureaucracy, receive the deference of many sectors of the com-

[39] Williams and Adrian, *op. cit.*, pp. 23–25 and ch. 9.

munity. Politics is not ordinarily pluralistic. Instead, its narrow structuring grants downtown merchants, chambers of commerce, and service associations the readiest access to official decision centers. With educational and class advantages widely distributed, the extensive scope of the government's responsibilities does sometimes elicit determined opposition; but even then the disputes tend to be issue oriented.[40]

A third type of polity attempts simply to "maintain traditional services." Its theme is that government do only what is absolutely necessary and avoid imposing tax burdens upon residents. In this context communications with government officials (and among non-government actors, too) are likely to be quite personalized. Concomitantly, the elected council, with its errand-boy roles, is held in low esteem, and the bureaucracy usually possesses little *esprit de corps.*

Some problems deliberately avoided by local officialdom may be passed along to higher government levels or handled by small cliques to which the community's businessmen and newspaper editors customarily belong. In either event relatively few people participate in most decisions, and those who do comprise a largely structured set. On occasion, though, intensity of feeling about matters that threaten the dominant ethos may induce sharp conflicts.[41]

The fourth and last category of local political norms encompasses those cities in which "arbitrating among conflicting interests" provides the chief value. While the government does not pursue any unidirectional policy and may remain largely neutral, its role is not inconsequential. Indeed, political leaders seem preoccupied with integrating competing demands within the community.

For this reason, a large and varied set of claimants may have considerable access to government, with no clearly specifiable subset of them emerging predominate. Indeed, interest aggregates that are nearly silent in other normative settings often take a legitimate part in arbiter politics, though their activity is frequently episodic and channeled informally. In this vortex of conflicting activity, decisions by government are often delayed, and sometimes they are put off indefinitely.[42]

These four descriptions of community ethics, drawn directly or freely extrapolated from the Williams and Adrian discussions, allow us to formulate several hypotheses about decision processes in cities with varying self-images and corresponding government functions. Some of the suppositions are also congruent with our own findings in Chapter V. In many notable respects, for example, Chicago politics illustrates an arbiter norm,

[40] *Ibid.,* pp. 25–27 and ch. 10.
[41] *Ibid.,* pp. 27–28 and ch. 11.
[42] *Ibid.,* pp. 28–29 and ch. 12.

Beloit fits the caretaker classification, and Detroit resembles best a growth model.

1. Communication rates over the time span of an issue controversy should fluctuate least in amenities and caretaker cities and most in arbiter cities. Furthermore, growth-centered locales may show considerable activity quite early in cases, while in arbiter communities interactions are likely to cluster in the third and fourth quartiles.
2. The varieties of participating actor roles, and the complements of individuals who play them, are probably largest in arbiter communities and smallest in caretaker ones, with amenities and growth cities taking an intermediary position.
3. Certain actor categories are likely to be conspicuously present or absent, depending upon the particular community norm stressed. Thus, economic actors, though prominent in all four cities, probably least dominate those emphasizing an arbiter function. In that locale, non-economic interests should participate widely, with their rate falling away in amenities and caretaker cities and reaching its lowest level in growth communities. Civic groups should be noteworthy in all except caretaker cities; conversely, political parties should be highly visible participants only in an arbiter setting. Finally, government personnel are probably most active in an amenities environment and least so in a caretaker one. If one looks solely at government bureaucracy, however, growth and amenities cities would bear close resemblance.
4. Interactions with governments in other jurisdictions should be highest in growth cities and lowest in those with a caretaker emphasis.
5. Full permeability should frequently characterize the interactions of arbiter communities. Though not uncommon in caretaker cities either, it is probably far less usual there than is impermeability. Fully permeable communications probably occur even less often in growth locales. As for issues in amenities cities, the preponderance of their interactions should exhibit partial permeability.
6. Formality is likely most apparent in amenities and growth locales and least apparent in arbiter and caretaker ones.
7. Regular interactions are probably most frequently found in cases set in an amenities or caretaker milieu. Growth communities, by contrast, are likely to exhibit considerable case patterning in their activities, and arbiter cities, many ephemeral interactions. The level of affect-laden communications should be proportional to the extent of non-regularity, with the highest degrees found in communities emphasizing arbiter functions.

INTERACTION AND THE DISTRIBUTION OF POWER

As a last illustration, we examine some implications that contrasting patterns of community power hold for decision processes. In raising this topic we are immediately faced with a difficult problem—and for political science a rather unusual one. We can quickly be overwhelmed by the plethora of available studies and critiques, their methodological diversity, and their apparently frequent contradictory conclusions.[43] Fortunately, the aims of this chapter do not require us to reevaluate the research procedures employed by various students of community power or to rate the plausibility of their diverse findings.[44] It is sufficient here to select from the literature one broad classification of community power and then to infer from it some derivative hypotheses.

Different social scientists suggest, of course, various typologies of community power. Dahl, for example, sets forth a list of five patterns: "covert integration by Economic Notables," "an executive-centered 'grand coalition of coalitions,' " "a coalition of chieftains," "independent sovereignties with spheres of influence," and "rival sovereignties fighting it out."[45] Except for the first, all these patterns supposedly have obtained in New Haven during one recent mayoral regime or another or have applied there simultaneously in different issue areas.[46] Miller identifies five configurations, too, with such quasi-geometric shapes as pyramids, cones, and blocks.[47] Rossi employs a four-part classification: pyramidal, caucus rule, polylith, and amorphous.[48] Agger and associates also construct a four-fold typology, with their categories labelled consensual mass, consensual elite, competitive mass, and competitive elite.[49]

[43] A recent comprehensive review of the field may be found in Arnold M. Rose, *The Power Structure* (New York: Oxford University Press, 1967), ch. 8. The first part (pp. 255–80) focuses on methodology, the second (pp. 280–97), on what Rose calls "theoretical and substantive issues." The comparative brevity of the latter should not be overinterpreted, for variations in theoretically relevant conclusions correlate noticeably with the kinds of investigative procedures employed. See also Nelson W. Polsby, *Community Power and Political Theory* (New Haven: Yale University Press, 1963).

[44] If a superabundance of case materials were available, one might utilize for this purpose a logic similar to that in Raoul Naroll, *Data Quality Control* (Glencoe: Free Press, 1962). As we remarked in Chapter V, however, few persons write about the same locale or topic.

[45] Robert A. Dahl, *Who Governs?* (New Haven: Yale University Press, 1961), ch. 15. No claim is made that his list is totally inclusive. "The number of theoretically possible patterns of integration is almost infinite"; "the likelihood of finding still other patterns could not be excluded a priori" (pp. 184 and 189).

[46] *Ibid.*, p. 189. Supporting evidence is provided in chs. 16–18. What might be called *overt* integration by economic notables did occur in New Haven at a far earlier time, though the notables were not just economically dominant (*ibid.*, ch. 2).

[47] Cited in Rose, *op. cit.*, p. 287. Rose also alludes to multi-model statements by D'Antonio and Form and by Barth.

[48] Rossi, *op. cit.*

[49] Agger, Goldrich and Swanson, *op. cit.*, ch. 3.

Even fairly complex typologies of local power, though, tend to reduce to simple pairs of alternatives. The four patterns in New Haven are all variants of "pluralistic democracy," while the rejected covert integration hypothesis involves focused elite assumptions. Similarly, Rossi's four classifications rapidly become three, amorphous being merely a "logical residual category" with no actual referents; and the three become two, since pyramidal and caucus-rule structures are basically similar, their sole difference relating to minor distinctions in the number of decision-makers who share power.

What remains in all the typologies is a contrast between cohesive, restricted power centers on the one hand, and looser, multi-nucleated influence structures on the other. The language used to describe this contrast may vary. Polsby, for example, distinguishes stratification theory from the pluralistic alternative. Our use hereafter of Rossi's terms—pyramidal and polylithic—is not to imply, therefore, that his analytic scheme is deemed superior to others, but only that he provides us two useful and familiar polar types.[50]

In pyramidal cities, community-wide issues are determined by a relatively small group of men, most of them of high status. This elite tends to be quite stable from decision to decision. Leaders in business and industry ordinarily stand at the apex of power, either because local homogeneity does not facilitate the emergence of countervailing political power or because, even in a diverse setting, they possess great authority and favored instruments for monitoring and intervening in the city's activities. In either sort of community, members of the elite are in general agreement about the best courses of action to be followed.

A subordinate level, composed of government and civic officials, executes the policy lines set by the top leadership. Together, these two highest strata nearly monopolize the decisional skills and political resources of the city. Politics in a pyramidal community is thus decidedly un-pluralistic: power is not widely shared and policies do not reflect major compromises. Nor is the issue process highly public. The initial determination of policies ordinarily occurs under private and informal conditions, even if subsequent steps are highly formalized and legalistic. Similarly, visible conflict is usually avoided, though massive public reactions occasionally ensue.

Polylithic cities, in contrast, show many clusters of power, with community affairs fashioned by shifting coalitions of actors. Ordinarily, most individuals or groups are without stakes in most issues; nor would their skills and resources allow them wholly general roles anyway. Thus,

[50] That much of the case literature seems to come from rather polylithic communities does not diminish the utility of the analytic contrast.

participants active on one issue area are usually absent or lacking in prominence on others.

The only sector of a polylithic community to participate generally in a wide range of decisions is its appointed and elected high government officialdom.[51] Businessmen, to be sure, still command considerable respect in many areas of the city's life, and they also frequently dominate service organizations and eleemosynary agencies. But often even they are in agreement on only a few issues. Moreover, in larger cities especially, heterogeneity permits alternate centers of power to emerge around political machines, voluntary associations, ethnic and labor groups, and other aggregates of lower class or lower status populations. In Rossi's words:

> . . . the leaders of the dominant economic institutions ordinarily wield power, but they are forced to take others into account when popular democratic rules allow the lower levels of the community an opportunity to place their representatives in public office.[52]

These two brief accounts of community power distributions, the pyramidal and the polylithic,[53] suggest the following hypotheses:

1. Interaction rates through time on a given issue should be more uniform in pyramidal than polylithic locales. Heterogeneous pyramidal cities, however, may show fairly marked upswings during the fourth quartile, as the details of what has already been decided are revealed to outsiders and they perhaps mount last-minute attempts to forestall outcomes. Polylithic communities, by contrast, should often exhibit observable declines in activity early in issue controversies and sizeable increases somewhat later.
2. Public statements by persons in the top echelon are unlikely in pyramidal communities, and those by second-level leaders are only a little more common. Furthermore, what public statements they do issue probably cluster in the fourth quartile.
3. The participant range should be narrow in pyramidal settings, with business the most frequent actor and specific individuals reappearing often enough to define a small number of cliques. In

[51] For example, in New Haven "only three leaders initiated or vetoed policies in more than one issue area. These were Lee, Logue, and Celentano." Dahl, *op. cit.,* p. 181 (italics omitted). Lee and Celentano were mayors of New Haven; Logue was development administrator.

[52] Rossi, *op. cit.,* p. 399.

[53] The descriptions draw upon materials in Rossi, Polsby, and Rose (cited above) as well as in the books about Syracuse, Chicago, New York City, and Oberlin referred to in Chapter V (notes 9, 11, 12, and 14). In the background, of course, are the fundamental constructs of Floyd Hunter and Robert A. Dahl.

polylithic communities the participant cost should be more diversified, with government officials usually on stage and non-government actors varying in prominence according to issue areas. Under these conditions small cliques are probably not apparent, though looser constellations may be.

4. Issue controversies in pyramidal cities likely involve few communications with external actors, while the existence of numerous participants in polylithic cities should encourage communications with allied and related interests outside the local setting.
5. Interactions in pyramidal locales are probably often impermeable. This should hold especially true for meetings that include members of dominant cliques and for the earlier messages they initiate. In polylithic settings, however, partial permeability is likely to predominate. Though impermeable meetings should still be far more common than fully permeable sessions, openness would also characterize the community, because of its continually high incidence of public statements.
6. Cases from pyramidal cities likely show somewhat heightened proportions of informal interactions, and particularly of informal meetings. Most meetings in polylithic communities, by contrast, should be formal, though they may occur within a matrix of informal intra-organizational, and especially intragovernmental, messages.
7. Regular communications should dominate cases in pyramidal cities. Considerable case-patterning, though, may occur if the issue falls outside the range of decisions familiar to the top elite. Ephemeral interactions are probably infrequent, except perhaps during the final quartile in more heterogeneous settings. In polylithic cities the rate of regular communications should be somewhat reduced. Case-patterning should also be common, since different sets of participants enter different issue areas. The openness of the system may also permit many ephemeral interactions throughout the time span of cases.

The various process statements we have applied to concepts of power, norms, and institutions in American cities are by necessity preliminary sketches. Moreover, the scope of our account has been narrowed by a considerable overlap in the phenomena described by those three orientations. Indeed, making process aspects explicit has probably helped draw attention to elements in common. Validation and elaboration of the specific hypotheses advanced above, however, must await the availability of more materials directly relevant to interaction analysis. As stated earlier, the greatest need is for additional case narratives.

There is, to be sure, no single and exclusively correct approach to the study of community decision-making. Hopefully, though, this volume has demonstrated that definitions and descriptions of case interaction units can avoid static representations of process. Because our methods highlight an important but often obscured dimension, they should usefully supplement more traditional ways of viewing metropolitan decisions.

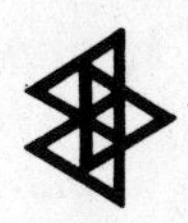

APPENDIX

The Code Employed in Analysis of Metropolitan Case Studies

A. Interaction mode
   1. Meeting (encounter, session)
   2. Message (communique)
   3. Public statement
B. Actor role (relevant organizational affiliation)
   1. Elected city
   2. Appointed city
   3. Elected county
   4. Appointed county
   5. Elected suburban
   6. Appointed suburban
   7. State
   8. Local intergovernmental
   9. Federal
   10. School
   11. Court
   12. Other governmental
   13. Governmentally appointed planning and sounding board
   14. Party functionary
   15. Business
   16. Labor
   17. Professional
   18. Communications
   19. Religion
   20. Civil rights
   21. Civic

22. *Ad hoc*
23. Other interest group
24. Non-affiliated
25. Unspecified

N.B. Encodings are made for each role included in a given interaction. Ordinarily, an individual is classified in only a single way. Codes 10 and 11 have precedence over any earlier code; codes 12, 23, 24, and 25 are residual. Such experts as lawyers, who speak for some interest, are identified with that code category rather than with their own profession. The words "city," "county," "suburban," and "state" refer only to the metropolitan area focused upon in a case. Other cities, counties, suburbs, and states are coded as "other governmental."

C. Spatial location
   1. In the metropolitan area
   2. Elsewhere in the state
   3. Outside the state
   4. Indeterminate

D. Permeability
   1. Impermeable
   2. Partly permeable
   3. Fully permeable

E. Formality
   1. Formal
   2. Informal

F. Continuity
   1. Regular
   2. Case patterned
   3. Ephemeral

G. Temporal position
   1. Before the first quartile
   2. First quartile
   3. Second quartile
   4. Third quartile
   5. Fourth quartile
   6. After the fourth quartile

INDEX

Printed in U.S.A.